Solicitors' Accounts Manual

12TH EDITION

Other titles available from Law Society Publishing:

SRA Handbook
Solicitors Regulation Authority

Titles from Law Society Publishing can be ordered from all good bookshops or direct (telephone 0870 850 1422, email **lawsociety@prolog.uk.com** or visit our online shop at **www.lawsociety.org.uk/bookshop**).

SOLICITORS' ACCOUNTS MANUAL

12TH EDITION

Solicitors Regulation Authority

The Law Society

© The Law Society 2011

ISBN: 978-1-907698-19-4

Crown copyright material is reproduced with the permission of the Controller of Her Majesty's Stationery Office

1st edition 1986
2nd edition 1987
3rd edition 1990
4th edition 1992
5th edition 1994
6th edition 1996
7th edition 1999
8th edition 2001
9th edition 2004
10th edition 2008
11th edition 2009

This 12th edition published in 2011 by the Law Society
113 Chancery Lane, London WC2A 1PL

Typeset by Columns Design XML Ltd, Reading
Printed by TJ International Ltd, Padstow, Cornwall

FSC
www.fsc.org
MIX
Paper from
responsible sources
FSC® C013056

The paper used for the text pages of this book is FSC certified. FSC (the Forest Stewardship Council) is an international network to promote responsible management of the world's forests.

Contents

Preface

INTRODUCTION

This is the 12th edition of the *Solicitors' Accounts Manual*. It contains a summary of the professional requirements in relation to the handling of client money.

The Solicitors' Accounts Rules 1998 were repealed on 6 October 2011 and replaced with the SRA Accounts Rules 2011 (Accounts Rules). The form and content of the Accounts Rules will be familiar to readers, but a number of significant changes have been made.

Amendments have been made to facilitate the introduction of outcomes-focused regulation (OFR) and alternative business structures (ABSs). OFR focuses on the ten high level Principles (contained in Part 2 of this Manual). They are mandatory, and underpin all aspects of regulation, including the Accounts Rules. A firm's first point of reference when considering compliance with the rules must always be the Principles.

The rules now govern practice both in England and Wales, and overseas. The rules have also been modernised and updated where appropriate, including renumbering throughout. The mandatory parts of the notes have been moved to the rules, and the remaining guidance notes are no longer binding.

Parts 1–6 of the Accounts Rules apply to practice carried on from an office in England and Wales. Part 7 applies to practice carried on from an office outside England and Wales.

The Accounts Rules are contained in Part 1 of this Manual and state the position as at 6 October 2011.

Principles and purpose of the Accounts Rules

A new introduction notes the application of the SRA Handbook Principles to the handling of client money and lists those which are particularly relevant to the Accounts Rules. It also notes the desired outcomes, and includes a general note on application of the rules.

PRACTICE IN ENGLAND AND WALES

Rule 1 has been expanded to state the overarching objective to keep client money safe. Compliance is required with the Principles set out in the SRA Handbook, and the outcomes in Chapter 7 of the SRA Code of Conduct (also contained in Part 2 of this Manual) relating to the effective financial management of the firm. The underlying principles specific to the Accounts Rules are unchanged.

Application

The rules in Parts 1–6 (England and Wales) apply to "you" as defined. They have been extended to cover ABSs (licensed bodies), and their managers and employees, in addition to the persons governed by the 1998 rules.

Definitions

Defined terms throughout the rules continue to be shown in italics.

New definitions for ABSs, and specifically for multi-disciplinary practices (MDPs) and "out-of-scope money", have been included to cover the position when the Law Society is designated as a licensing authority.

Compliance Officer for Finance and Administration

Rule 6 of the Accounts Rules continues to require all principals to ensure accounts rules compliance but extends that duty to the Compliance Officer for Finance and Administration (COFA), whether a manager or non-manager. Under rule 8.5(e) of the SRA Authorisation Rules 2011, the COFA must keep a record of any failure to comply for production to the Solicitors Regulation Authority (SRA) on request, and also report any breaches to the SRA.

Outcomes-focused regulation

The Accounts Rules necessarily remain prescriptive but OFR has been introduced in the two areas of withdrawals from client account and interest.

Withdrawals from client account (rule 21 of the Accounts Rules and paragraph 4 of the SRA Guidelines – Accounting Procedures and Systems at Appendix 3)

The rules no longer prescribe who may authorise a withdrawal from client account, and firms must establish appropriate systems and procedures for withdrawals from client account (rule 21.1 to 21.2, guidance note (i) to rule 21, and paragraph 4 of the Guidelines). An exception to the OFR approach is that non-manager owners and non-employee owners are not permitted to be signatories.

Electronic signatures for withdrawals from client account are now permitted, subject to suitable safeguards and controls (rule 21.1 and paragraph 4.4 of the Guidelines).

Interest (rules 22 to 25)

The previously detailed interest provisions have been replaced with four basic requirements:

- to pay interest when it is fair and reasonable to do so in all the circumstances – rule 22.1;
- to pay a fair and reasonable sum – rule 23;
- to have a written interest policy, the terms of which must be drawn to the attention of clients – rule 22.3 and guidance note (ii)(a); and
- to act fairly when entering into an agreement to contract out of the payment of interest, including the provision of sufficient information at the outset to enable the client to give informed consent– rule 25.2.

Complaints on interest are dealt with by the Legal Ombudsman but the obligation to have an interest policy, and to draw it to the attention of clients, should help to manage expectations and lead to a reduction in complaints (guidance notes (i)(c) and (vi)(a) to rule 22).

The "interest table" (referring to amounts and length of time held) and the £20 de minimis have been removed, but the other circumstances where interest is not payable have been retained (rule 22.2). The non-payment of interest on money held for counsel's fees, if counsel requests a delay in settlement, has been extended to any professional disbursement.

Principals who do not receive or pay interest due to their religious beliefs may contract out but transparency is essential (guidance note (iii) to rule 25).

Factors to consider in setting an interest policy are set out in guidance notes (i)(a) to (i), (ii)(a), (iii)(a), (iv)(a) and (v)(a) to rule 22. Factors to consider when calculating interest are set out in guidance notes (i)-(vii) to rule 23.

Although the Legal Services Act 2007 has removed the distinction between interest earned on client money held in a general client account and on that held in a separate designated client account, the tax regime means that firms wishing to retain any part of the interest earned on client money will need to hold that money in the general client account (guidance note (i)(d) to rule 22).

The 1998 interest provisions will continue to apply to all existing client matters as at 5 October 2011, including the inability to contract out of paying interest for religious reasons. The new provisions will apply in respect of new clients from 6 October 2011, and for new matters for existing clients opened on or after that date.

Alternative business structures

The application of the rules to licensed bodies will take effect, as described below, from the designation of the Law Society as a licensing authority.

Application

The rules apply to licensed bodies and their managers and employees. However, in the case of an MDP, the rules apply only in respect of those activities for which the MDP is regulated by the SRA (rule 4.2 and guidance note (v)). For an explanation of MDPs, see below.

Multi-disciplinary practices

MDPs are licensed bodies providing a range of different services, some only of which are regulated by the SRA. An MDP is required to ringfence client money arising from its SRA-regulated activities.

Money arising from an MDP's non-SRA regulated activities is defined as "out-of-scope money". The rules do not apply to this type of money, save to the limited extent specified (rule 12.1).

As money arising from non-SRA regulated activities is not client money for the purposes of the Accounts Rules, it should not normally be paid into the client account. It could be paid into an office account of the firm or into an account for holding money regulated by another regulator (see the expanded definition of "office account").

The receipt of out-of-scope money which is mixed with other types of money is dealt with in rules 17 (receipt of costs) and 18 (mixed payments). Any out-of-scope money must be transferred out of the client account within 14 days of receipt (rules 17.1(a) and (c), 17.4 and 18.3, guidance note (xi) to rule 17 and guidance note (iii) to rule 18).

Guidance note (xi) to rule 29 sets out the general position in relation to record keeping for MDPs. See also rules 29.15 and 29.17(b)(iv).

Client account

Section 85 of the Solicitors Act 1974 protects the client account of a "traditional" firm against the bank at which the money is held. Equivalent statutory protection is being sought for the client accounts of an ABS; in the meantime, an ABS must have a contractual arrangement with its bank to provide similar protection for its client account (rule 13.6 and guidance note (iii)).

An ABS must inform its clients if it is (or becomes) owned by a bank or building society (or other bank or building society in the same group) at which its client account is held (rule 13.7).

Clarificatory and updating changes

A provision has been included to make clear that bank statements must be obtained at least every five weeks (rule 29.11), and electronic bank statements are now permitted (rules 29.11(b) and 30.3).

Reconciliations must be carried out at least once every five weeks in all cases. The extended 14 week period for passbook-operated separate designated client accounts held by solicitor-trustees has been removed (rule 29.12).

The electronic signing and delivery of bills, which is a matter of law, is referred to in guidance note (ix) to rule 17.

The requirement to distinguish between fees, paid disbursements and unpaid disbursements on bills has been removed as this too is a matter of law (guidance note (vii) to rule 29).

A new provision has been included to cover the position when a damages cheque, made payable to a client, is paid into the client account under the Law Society's Conditional Fee Agreement. This sum becomes client money on payment into the client account but the costs element must be transferred out of the client account within 14 days of receipt (rules 12.5, 14.2(e) and 17.1(e)).

The naming requirements for the client accounts of a sole practitioner, partnership and incorporated practice have been clarified (rule 13.3(a)-(c)). A new provision has been added to cover the naming of a client account where trustees comprise a sole practitioner and/or his or her employees (rule 13.3(f)).

Binding provisions moved from the notes to the rules include:

- the requirement not to provide banking facilities through a client account – rule 14.5 and guidance note (v);
- the position on misdirected electronic payments or other direct transfers from clients or paying third parties – rule 17.6;
- the prohibition on round sum withdrawals on account of costs – rule 17.7;
- the requirement to keep the original bill or notification of costs on the file for a trust of which the only trustees are within the firm – rule 17.8;
- the prohibition on undrawn costs, which cannot be set off against any general shortage, remaining in a client account– rule 17.9;
- the requirement to show all shortages when preparing reconciliation statements – rule 29.14.

Guidance note (vii) to rule 17 gives an example of when costs are "properly" due under rule 17.2 and should be transferred out of the client account, and explains the rationale behind the rule. Guidance note (viii) to rule 17 explains what is meant by "earmarking" in rule 17.3, and deals with the issue where a firm wants to obtain clients' prior approval of its costs.

Guidance note (xii) to rule 17 cross-refers to the SRA Code of Conduct in relation to the need to ensure that bills reflect the actual amount spent on disbursements.

The legal aid provisions have been amended to reflect the current position on advance payments from the Legal Services Commission (rule 19.1(a) and guidance note (ii)).

A new guidance note (xi) to rule 21 distinguishes Land Registry application fees paid by "direct debit" from traditional direct debits and standing orders. The latter cannot be set up on a client account because of the need for a specific authority for each withdrawal.

A new guidance note (x) to rule 32 clarifies that an in-house lawyer, who only operates the non-solicitor employer's account, is not required to deliver an accountant's report.

Accountants' reports

An accountancy practice which has an ownership interest in, or is part of the group structure of, a licensed body is prohibited from preparing the accountant's report for that body (rule 34.2(a)(iii)).

The role of the reporting accountant in relation to the interest provisions is summarised in guidance notes (vii)(a)-(b) to rule 22. The accountant will continue to make limited checks under rule 42(1)(o) of the 1998 rules in respect of existing client matters taken on prior to 6 October 2011. The accountant is not required to check compliance with the 2011 interest provisions nor to determine the adequacy of a firm's interest policy (rule 41.1(d)). There is, however, a duty to report substantial departures from the Guidelines discovered whilst carrying out work in preparation of the report (rule 40, and paragraph 2.8 of the SRA Guidelines – Accounting Procedures and Systems at Appendix 3 which states the need for policies and systems for the payment of fair and reasonable interest).

Rule 39.1(c) includes a specific reference to the use of paid cheques when checking sample payments into and from client account (already included in the reporting accountant's checklist).

The requirement for an explanation of any significant difference between liabilities to clients and client money held has been moved from the notes to rule 44.

For an accounting period which straddles 6 October 2011, the reporting accountant will:

- check compliance with the Solicitors' Accounts Rules 1998 up to and including 5 October 2011; and
- check compliance with the SRA Accounts Rules 2011 from 6 October 2011.

OVERSEAS PRACTICE

Part 7 of the Accounts Rules applies to practice outside England and Wales. These provisions were previously contained in rules 15.15, 15.27 and 20.08 of the Solicitor's Code of Conduct 2007.

Rule 47 sets out the purpose of the overseas accounts rules; i.e. to ensure protection for client money similar to that afforded by the domestic rules, but by way of rules which are more adaptable to conditions in other jurisdictions.

Apart from extending the overseas accounts provisions to licensed bodies, few substantive changes have been made to the provisions previously set out in the Solicitors' Code of Conduct 2007.

The interest provisions at rule 49 refer to paying fair and reasonable interest on client money when it is fair and reasonable for interest to be earned. This replaces the previous reference to paying proper interest if interest ought, in fairness, to be earned, in order to reflect the new terminology in Parts 1-6 of the rules.

A specific six month time limit for delivery of a report has been inserted at rule 50.4 to reflect the current requirements for England and Wales.

Part 2 of this Manual contains the SRA Handbook Principles and extracts from the SRA Code of Conduct 2011 which relate to the keeping of accounts by solicitors.

The full text of the SRA Handbook, including the SRA Accounts Rules and the SRA Code of Conduct, can be found on the website of the Solicitors Regulation Authority at **www.sra.org.uk**.
September 2011

[1] Accounts Rules

[1.1] SRA Accounts Rules 2011

[Last updated 6 October 2011]

PREAMBLE

Authority: made by the Solicitors Regulation Authority Board under sections 32, 33A, 34, 37, 79 and 80 of the Solicitors Act 1974, section 9 of the Administration of Justice Act 1985, sections 83(5)(h) and 93 of, and paragraph 20 of Schedule 11 to, the Legal Services Act 2007 with the approval of the Legal Services Board;

date: 6 October 2011;

replacing: the Solicitors' Accounts Rules 1998;

regulating: the accounts of solicitors and their employees, registered European lawyers and their employees, registered foreign lawyers, recognised bodies and their managers and employees, and licensed bodies and their managers and employees, in respect of practice in England and Wales; and

regulating: the accounts of solicitors, lawyer-controlled bodies and their managers, lawyers of England and Wales who are managers of overseas law firms controlled by lawyers of England and Wales, solicitors who are named trustees, and managers of a lawyer-controlled body who are named trustees, in respect of practice outside the UK; and

regulating: the accounts of solicitors and registered European lawyers, lawyer-controlled and registered European lawyer-controlled bodies and their managers, lawyer of England and Wales and registered European lawyer managers of overseas law firms controlled by lawyers of England and Wales and/or registered European lawyers, solicitors and registered European lawyers who are named trustees, and managers of a lawyer-controlled body or a registered European lawyer-controlled body who are named trustees, in respect of practice from Scotland or Northern Ireland.

For the definition of words in italics in Parts 1–6 and 8, see rule 2 – Interpretation. For the definition of words in italics in Part 7 see rule 48 – Application and Interpretation (overseas provisions).

INTRODUCTION

The Principles set out in the Handbook apply to all aspects of practice, including the handling of client money. Those which are particularly relevant to these rules are that you must:

- protect client money and assets;

- act with integrity;

- behave in a way that maintains the trust the public places in you and in the provision of legal services;

- comply with your legal and regulatory obligations and deal with your regulators and ombudsmen in an open, timely and co-operative manner; and

- run your business or carry out your role in the business effectively and in accordance with proper governance and sound financial and risk management principles.

The desired outcomes which apply to these rules are that:

- client money is safe;

- clients and the public have confidence that client money held by firms will be safe;

- firms are managed in such a way, and with appropriate systems and procedures in place, so as to safeguard client money;

- client accounts are used for appropriate purposes only; and

- the SRA is aware of issues in a firm relevant to the protection of client money.

Underlying principles which are specific to the accounts rules are set out in rule 1 below.

These rules apply to all those who carry on or work in a firm and to the firm itself (see rules 4 and 5). In relation to a multi-disciplinary practice, the rules apply only in respect of those activities for which the practice is regulated by the SRA, and are concerned only with money handled by the practice which relates to those regulated activities.

PART 1: GENERAL

Rule 1: The overarching objective and underlying principles

1.1   The purpose of these rules is to keep *client money* safe. This aim must always be borne in mind in the application of these rules.

1.2   *You* must comply with the Principles set out in the Handbook, and the outcomes in Chapter 7 of the *SRA Code of Conduct* in relation to the effective financial management of the *firm*, and in particular must:

(a) keep other people's money separate from money belonging to *you* or *your firm*;

(b) keep other people's money safely in a *bank* or *building society* account identifiable as a *client account* (except when the rules specifically provide otherwise);

(c) use each *client's* money for that *client's* matters only;

(d) use money held as *trustee* of a *trust* for the purposes of that *trust* only;

(e) establish and maintain proper accounting systems, and proper internal controls over those systems, to ensure compliance with the rules;

(f) keep proper accounting records to show accurately the position with regard to the money held for each *client* and *trust*;

(g) account for *interest* on other people's money in accordance with the rules;

(h)   co-operate with the *SRA* in checking compliance with the rules; and

(i)   deliver annual accountant's reports as required by the rules.

Rule 2: Interpretation

2.1   The guidance notes do not form part of the rules.

2.2   In Parts 1 to 6 and 8 of these rules, unless the context otherwise requires:

accounting period has the meaning given in rule 33;

agreed fee has the meaning given in rule 17.5;

AJA means the Administration of Justice Act 1985;

approved regulator means any body listed as an approved regulator in paragraph 1 of Schedule 4 to the *LSA*, or designated as an approved regulator by an order under paragraph 17 of that Schedule;

authorised body means a body that has been authorised by the *SRA* to practise as a *licensed body* or a *recognised body*;

authorised non-SRA firm means a firm which is authorised to carry on *legal activities* by an *approved regulator* other than the *SRA*;

bank has the meaning given in section 87(1) of the *SA*;

building society means a building society within the meaning of the Building Societies Act 1986;

client means the person for whom *you* act;

client account has the meaning given in rule 13.2;

client money has the meaning given in rule 12;

COFA means the compliance officer for finance and administration in accordance with rule 8.5 of the *SRA Authorisation Rules*, and in relation to a *licensable body* is a reference to its Head of Finance and Administration within the meaning of the *LSA*;

Companies Acts means the Companies Act 1985 and the Companies Act 2006;

company means a company registered under the *Companies Acts*, an *overseas* company incorporated in an *Establishment Directive state* and registered under the Companies Act 1985 and/or the Companies Act 2006 or a *societas Europaea*;

costs means *your fees* and *disbursements*;

Court of Protection deputy includes a deputy who was appointed by the Court of Protection as a receiver under the Mental Health Act 1983 before the commencement date of the Mental Capacity Act 2005;

director means a director of a *company*; and in relation to a *societas Europaea* includes:

(i) in a two-tier system, a member of the management organ and a member of the supervisory organ; and

(ii) in a one-tier system, a member of the administrative organ;

disbursement means, in respect of those activities for which the practice is regulated by the *SRA*, any sum spent or to be spent on behalf of the *client* or *trust* (including any VAT element);

Establishment Directive means the Establishment of Lawyers Directive 98/5/EC;

Establishment Directive profession means any profession listed in Article 1.2(a) of the *Establishment Directive*, including a solicitor, barrister or advocate of the *UK*;

Establishment Directive state means a state to which the *Establishment Directive* applies;

fees means *your* own charges or profit costs (including any VAT element);

firm means an *authorised body*, a *recognised sole practitioner* or a body or person which should be authorised by the *SRA* as a *recognised body* or *recognised sole practitioner* (but which could not be authorised by another *approved regulator*), but can also include in-house practice;

general client account has the meaning given in rule 13.5(b);

interest includes a sum in lieu of interest;

lawyer means a member of one of the following professions, entitled to practise as such:

(i) the profession of solicitor, barrister, or advocate of the *UK*;

(ii) a profession whose members are authorised to carry on *legal activities* by an *approved regulator* other than the *SRA*;

(iii) an *Establishment Directive profession* other than a *UK* profession;

(iv) a legal profession which has been approved by the *SRA* for the purpose of *recognised bodies* in England and Wales; and

(v) any other regulated legal profession specified by the *SRA* for the purpose of this definition;

legal activity has the meaning given in section 12 of the *LSA* and includes any *reserved legal activity* and any other activity which consists of the provision of legal advice or assistance, or representation in connection with the application of the law or resolution of legal disputes;

licensable body means a body which meets the criteria in rule 14 (Eligibility criteria and fundamental requirements for licensed bodies) of the *SRA Practice Framework Rules*;

licensed body means a body licensed by the *SRA* under Part 5 of the *LSA*;

licensing authority means an *approved regulator* which is designated as a licensing authority under Part 1 of Schedule 10 to the *LSA*, and whose licensing rules have been approved for the purposes of the *LSA*;

LLP means a limited liability partnership incorporated under the Limited Liability Partnerships Act 2000;

local authority means any of those bodies which are listed in section 270 of the Local Government Act 1972 or in section 21(1) of the Local Government and Housing Act 1989;

LSA means the Legal Services Act 2007;

manager means:

  (i)   a member of an *LLP*;

  (ii) a *director* of a *company*;

  (iii) a *partner* in a *partnership*; or

  (iv) in relation to any other body, a member of its governing body;

MDP means a *licensed body* which is a multi-disciplinary practice providing a range of different services, some only of which are regulated by the *SRA*;

mixed payment has the meaning given in rule 18.1;

non-solicitor employer means any employer other than a *recognised body*, *recognised sole practitioner*, *licensed body* or *authorised non-SRA firm*;

office account means an account of the *firm* for holding *office money* and/or *out-of-scope money*, or other means of holding *office money* or *out-of-scope money* (for example, the office cash box or an account holding money regulated by a regulator other than the *SRA*);

office money has the meaning given in rule 12;

out-of-scope money means money held or received by an *MDP* in relation to those activities for which it is not regulated by the *SRA*;

overseas means outside England and Wales;

partner means a person who is or is held out as a partner in a *partnership*;

partnership means an unincorporated body in which persons are or are held out as *partners*, and does not include a body incorporated as an *LLP*;

principal means:

  (i)   a *sole practitioner*;

  (ii) a *partner* in a *partnership*;

  (iii) in the case of a *recognised body* which is an *LLP* or *company*, the *recognised body* itself;

  (iv) in the case of a *licensed body* which is an *LLP* or *company*, the *licensed body* itself;

(v)   the principal *solicitor* or *REL* (or any one of them) employed by a *non-solicitor employer* (for example, in a law centre or in commerce and industry); or

(vi)   in relation to any other body, a member of its governing body;

private loan means a loan other than one provided by an institution which provides loans on standard terms in the normal course of its activities;

professional disbursement means, in respect of those activities for which the practice is regulated by the *SRA*, the fees of counsel or other *lawyer*, or of a professional or other agent or expert instructed by *you*, including the fees of interpreters, translators, process servers, surveyors and estate agents but not travel agents' charges;

recognised body means a body recognised by the *SRA* under section 9 of the *AJA*;

recognised sole practitioner means a *solicitor* or *REL* authorised by the *SRA* under section 1B of the *SA* to practise as a *sole practitioner*;

regular payment has the meaning given in rule 19;

REL means registered European lawyer, namely, an individual registered with the *SRA* under regulation 17 of the European Communities (Lawyer's Practice) Regulations 2000 (S.I. 2000 no. 1119);

reserved legal activity has the meaning given in section 12 of the *LSA*, and includes the exercise of a right of audience, the conduct of litigation, reserved instrument activities, probate activities, notarial activities and the administration of oaths, as defined in Schedule 2 to the *LSA*;

RFL means registered foreign lawyer, namely, an individual registered with the *SRA* under section 89 of the Courts and Legal Services Act 1990;

SA means the Solicitors Act 1974;

separate designated client account has the meaning given in rule 13.5(a);

societas Europaea means a European public limited liability *company* within the meaning of Article 1 of Council Regulation 2157/2001/EC;

Society means the Law Society, in accordance with section 87 of the *SA*;

sole practitioner means a *solicitor* or *REL* practising as a sole principal, and does not include a *solicitor* or *REL* practising in-house;

solicitor means a person who has been admitted as a solicitor of the Senior Courts of England and Wales and whose name is on the roll kept by the *Society* under section 6 of the *SA*;

SRA means the Solicitors Regulation Authority, and reference to the SRA as an *approved regulator* or *licensing authority* means the SRA carrying out regulatory functions assigned to the *Society* as an *approved regulator* or *licensing authority*;

SRA Authorisation Rules means the SRA Authorisation Rules for Legal Services Bodies and Licensable Bodies 2011;

SRA Code of Conduct means the SRA Code of Conduct 2011;

SRA Practice Framework Rules means the SRA Practice Framework Rules 2011;

statutory undertakers means:

(i) any persons authorised by any enactment to carry on any railway, light railway, tramway, road transport, water transport, canal, inland navigation, dock, harbour, pier or lighthouse undertaking or any undertaking for the supply of hydraulic power; and

(ii) any licence holder within the meaning of the Electricity Act 1989, any public gas supplier, any water or sewerage undertaker, the Environment Agency, any public telecommunications operator, the Post Office, the Civil Aviation Authority and any relevant airport operator within the meaning of Part V of the Airports Act 1986;

trustee includes a personal representative (i.e. an executor or an administrator), and "trust" includes the duties of a personal representative;

UK means United Kingdom;

without delay means, in normal circumstances, either on the day of receipt or on the next working day; and

you means:

(i) a *solicitor*; or

(ii) an *REL*;

in either case who is:

(A) a *sole practitioner*;

(B) a *partner* in a *partnership* which is a *recognised body, licensed body* or *authorised non-SRA firm* or in a *partnership* which should be a *recognised body* but has not been recognised by the *SRA*;

(C) an assistant, associate, professional support lawyer, consultant, locum or person otherwise employed in the practice of a *recognised body, licensed body, recognised sole practitioner* or *authorised non-SRA firm*; or of a *partnership* which should be a *recognised body* but has not been recognised by the *SRA*, or of a *sole practitioner* who should be a *recognised sole practitioner* but has not been authorised by the *SRA*; and "employed" in this context shall be interpreted in accordance with the definition of "employee" for the purposes of the *SRA Code of Conduct*;

(D) employed as an in-house lawyer by a *non-solicitor employer* (for example, in a law centre or in commerce and industry);

(E) a *director* of a *company* which is a *recognised body, licensed body* or *authorised non-SRA firm*, or of a *company* which is a *manager* of a *recognised body, licensed body* or *authorised non-SRA firm*;

(F)   a member of an *LLP* which is a *recognised body*, *licensed body* or *authorised non-SRA firm*, or of an *LLP* which is a *manager* of a *recognised body*, *licensed body* or *authorised non-SRA firm*; or

(G)   a *partner* in a *partnership* with separate legal personality which is a *manager* of a *recognised body*, *licensed body* or *authorised non-SRA firm*;

(iii)   an *RFL* practising:

     (A)   as a *partner* in a *partnership* which is a *recognised body*, *licensed body* or *authorised non-SRA firm*, or in a *partnership* which should be a *recognised body* but has not been recognised by the *SRA*;

     (B)   as the *director* of a *company* which is a *recognised body*, *licensed body* or *authorised non-SRA firm*, or as the *director* of a *company* which is a *manager* of a *recognised body*, *licensed body* or *authorised non-SRA firm*;

     (C)   as a member of an *LLP* which is a *recognised body*, *licensed body* or *authorised non-SRA firm*, or as a member of an *LLP* which is a *manager* of a *recognised body*, *licensed body* or *authorised non-SRA firm*;

     (D)   as a *partner* in a *partnership* with separate legal personality which is a *manager* of a *recognised body*, *licensed body* or *authorised non-SRA firm*;

     (E)   as an employee of a *recognised body*, *licensed body* or *recognised sole practitioner*; or

     (F)   as an employee of a *partnership* which should be a *recognised body* but has not been authorised by the *SRA*, or of a *sole practitioner* who should be a *recognised sole practitioner* but has not been authorised by the *SRA*;

(iv)   a *recognised body*;

(v)   a *licensed body*;

(vi)   a *manager* or employee of a *recognised body* or *licensed body*, or of a *partnership* which should be a *recognised body* but has not been authorised by the *SRA*; or

(vii)   an employee of a *recognised sole practitioner*, or of a *sole practitioner* who should be a *recognised sole practitioner* but has not been authorised by the *SRA*;

and "you" includes "your" as appropriate;

the singular includes the plural and vice versa, and references to the masculine or feminine include the neuter.

Guidance notes

(i)   The effect of the definition of "you" in rule 2.2 is that the rules apply equally to all those who carry on or work in a firm and to the firm itself. See also rule 4 (persons governed by the rules) and rule 5 (persons exempt from the rules).

(ii)   The general definition of "office account" is wide (see rule 2.2). However, rule 17.1(b) (receipt and transfer of costs) and rule 19.1(b) and 19.2(b) (payments from the Legal Services Commission) specify that certain money is to be placed in an office account at a bank or building society. Out-of-scope money can be held in an office account (which could be an account regulated by another regulator); it must not be held in a client account.

(iii)   For a flowchart summarising the effect of the rules, see Appendix 1. For more details of the treatment of different types of money, see the chart "Special situations – what applies" at Appendix 2. These two appendices do not form part of the rules but are included to help solicitors and their staff find their way about the rules.

Rule 3: Geographical scope

3.1   Parts 1 to 6 of these rules apply to practice carried on from an office in England and Wales. Part 7 of these rules applies to practice carried on from an office outside England and Wales.

Rule 4: Persons governed by the rules

4.1   Save as provided in rule 4.2 below, Parts 1 to 6 of these rules apply to *you*.

4.2   In relation to an *MDP*, the rules apply to *you* only in respect of those activities for which the *MDP* is regulated by the *SRA*.

4.3   Part 6 of the rules (accountants' reports) also applies to reporting accountants.

4.4   If *you* have held or received *client money*, but no longer do so, whether or not *you* continue in practice, *you* continue to be bound by some of the rules.

Guidance notes

(i)   "You" is defined in rule 2.2. All employees of a recognised body or licensed body are directly subject to the rules, following changes made by the Legal Services Act 2007. All employees of a recognised sole practitioner are also directly subject to the rules under sections 1B and 34A of the Solicitors Act 1974. Non-compliance by any member of staff will also lead to the principals being in breach of the rules – see rule 6. Misconduct by an employee can also lead to an order of the SRA or the Solicitors Disciplinary Tribunal under section 43 of the Solicitors Act 1974 imposing restrictions on his or her employment.

(ii)   Rules which continue to apply to you where you no longer hold client money include:

[1.1] ACCOUNTS RULES

(a) rule 7 (duty to remedy breaches);

(b) rule 17.2 and 17.8, rule 29.15 to 29.24 and rule 30 (retention of records);

(c) rule 31 (production of records);

(d) Part 6 (accountants' reports), and in particular rule 32 and rule 33.5 (delivery of final report), and rule 35.2 and rule 43 (completion of checklist).

(iii)   The rules do not cover trusteeships carried on in a purely personal capacity outside any legal practice. It will normally be clear from the terms of the appointment whether you are being appointed in a purely personal capacity or in your professional capacity. If you are charging for the work, it is clearly being done in a professional capacity. Use of professional stationery may also indicate that the work is being done in a professional capacity.

(iv)   A solicitor who wishes to retire from private practice will need to make a decision about any professional trusteeship. There are three possibilities:

(a) continue to act as a professional trustee (as evidenced by, for instance, charging for work done, or by continuing to use the title "solicitor" in connection with the trust). In this case, the solicitor must continue to hold a practising certificate, and money subject to the trust must continue to be dealt with in accordance with the rules.

(b) continue to act as trustee, but in a purely personal capacity. In this case, the solicitor must stop charging for the work, and must not be held out as a solicitor (unless this is qualified by words such as "non-practising" or "retired") in connection with the trust.

(c) cease to be a trustee.

(v)   A licensed body may undertake a range of services, comprising both "traditional" legal services and other, related, services of a non-legal nature, for example, where a solicitor, estate agent and surveyor set up in practice together. Where a licensed body practises in this way (an MDP), only some of the services it provides (reserved and other legal activities, and other activities which are subject to one or more conditions on the body's licence) are within the regulatory reach of the SRA. Other, "non-legal", activities of the licensed body may be regulated by another regulator, and some activities may not fall within the regulatory ambit of any regulator.

Rule 5: Persons exempt from the rules

5.1   The rules do not apply to *you* when:

(a) practising as an employee of:

(i)   a *local authority*;

(ii)   *statutory undertakers*;

12 SOLICITORS' ACCOUNTS MANUAL (12TH EDITION)

(iii) a body whose accounts are audited by the Comptroller and Auditor General;

(iv) the Duchy of Lancaster;

(v) the Duchy of Cornwall; or

(vi) the Church Commissioners; or

(b) practising as the Solicitor of the City of London; or

(c) carrying out the functions of:

(i) a coroner or other judicial office; or

(ii) a sheriff or under-sheriff; or

(d) practising as a *manager* or employee of an *authorised non-SRA firm*, and acting within the scope of that *firm's* authorisation to practise.

Guidance note

(i) A person practising as a manager or employee of an authorised non-SRA firm is exempt from the Accounts Rules when acting within the scope of the firm's authorisation. Thus if a solicitor is a partner or employee in a firm authorised by the Council for Licensed Conveyancers, the rules will not apply to any money received by the solicitor in connection with conveyancing work. However if the solicitor does in-house litigation work – say collecting money owed to the firm – the Accounts Rules will apply to any money received by the solicitor in that context. This is because, whilst in-house litigation work is within the scope of the solicitor's authorisation as an individual, it is outside the scope of authorisation of the firm.

Rule 6: Principals' responsibility for compliance

6.1 All the *principals* in a *firm* must ensure compliance with the rules by the *principals* themselves and by everyone employed in the *firm*. This duty also extends to the *directors* of a *recognised body* or *licensed body* which is a *company*, or to the members of a *recognised body* or *licensed body* which is an *LLP*. It also extends to the *COFA* of a *firm* (whether a *manager* or non-*manager*).

Guidance note

(i) Rule 8.5(d) of the SRA Authorisation Rules requires all firms to have a COFA. The appointment of a COFA satisfies the requirement under section 92 of the Legal Services Act 2007 for a licensed body to appoint a Head of Finance and Administration. Under rule 6 of the accounts rules, the COFA must ensure compliance with the accounts rules. This obligation is in addition to, not instead of, the duty of all the principals to ensure compliance (the COFA may be subject to this duty both as COFA and as a principal). Under rule 8.5(e) of the SRA Authorisation Rules, the COFA must report any breaches of the accounts rules to the SRA as soon as reasonably practicable. (See also outcomes 10.3 and 10.4 of Chapter 10 of the SRA Code of Conduct in relation to the general duty to report serious financial difficulty or serious misconduct.)

Rule 7: Duty to remedy breaches

7.1   Any breach of the rules must be remedied promptly upon discovery. This includes the replacement of any money improperly withheld or withdrawn from a *client account*.

7.2   In a private practice, the duty to remedy breaches rests not only on the person causing the breach, but also on all the *principals* in the *firm*. This duty extends to replacing missing *client money* from the *principals'* own resources, even if the money has been misappropriated by an employee or another *principal*, and whether or not a claim is subsequently made on the *firm's* insurance or the Compensation Fund.

Rule 8: Liquidators, trustees in bankruptcy, Court of Protection deputies and trustees of occupational pension schemes

8.1   If in the course of practice *you* act as:

(a)   a liquidator,

(b)   a trustee in bankruptcy,

(c)   a *Court of Protection deputy*, or

(d)   a trustee of an occupational pension scheme which is subject to section 47(1)(a) of the Pensions Act 1995 (appointment of an auditor) and section 49(1) (separate bank account) and regulations under section 49(2)(b) (books and records),

you must comply with:

(i)   the appropriate statutory rules or regulations;

(ii)   the Principles referred to, and the underlying principles set out, in rule 1; and

(iii)   the requirements of rule 8.2 to 8.4 below;

and will then be deemed to have satisfactorily complied with the Accounts Rules.

8.2   In respect of any records kept under the appropriate statutory rules, there must also be compliance with:

(a)   rule 29.15 – bills and notifications of costs;

(b)   rule 29.17(c) – retention of records;

(c)   rule 29.20 – centrally kept records;

(d)   rule 31 – production of records; and

(e)   rule 39.1(l) and (p) – reporting accountant to check compliance.

8.3   If a liquidator or trustee in bankruptcy uses any of the *firm's client accounts* for holding money pending transfer to the Insolvency Services Account or to a local bank account authorised by the Secretary of State, he or she must comply with the Accounts Rules in all respects whilst the money is held in the *client account*.

8.4 If the appropriate statutory rules or regulations do not govern the holding or receipt of *client money* in a particular situation (for example, money below a certain limit), *you* must comply with the Accounts Rules in all respects in relation to that money.

Guidance notes

(i) The Insolvency Regulations 1994 (S.I. 1994 no. 2507) regulate liquidators and trustees in bankruptcy.

(ii) The Court of Protection Rules 2007 (S.I. 2007 no. 1744 (L.12)) regulate Court of Protection deputies (see rule 2.2).

(iii) Money held or received by liquidators, trustees in bankruptcy, Court of Protection deputies and trustees of occupational pension schemes is client money but, because of the statutory rules and rule 8.1, it will not normally be kept in a client account. If for any reason it is held in a client account, the Accounts Rules apply to that money for the time it is so held (see rule 8.3 and 8.4).

Rule 9: Joint accounts

9.1 If, when acting in a *client's* matter, *you* hold or receive money jointly with the *client*, another practice or another third party, the rules in general do not apply, but the following must be complied with:

(a) rule 29.11 – statements from banks, building societies and other financial institutions;

(b) rule 29.15 – bills and notifications of costs;

(c) rule 29.17(b)(ii) – retention of statements and passbooks;

(d) rule 29.21 – centrally kept records;

(e) rule 31 – production of records; and

(f) rule 39.1(m) and (p) – reporting accountant to check compliance.

A joint account is not a *client account* but money held in a joint account is *client money*.

Operation of the joint account by you only

9.2 If the joint account is operated only by *you*, *you* must ensure that *you* receive the statements from the *bank*, *building society* or other financial institution in accordance with rule 29.11, and have possession of any passbooks.

Shared operation of the joint account

9.3 If *you* share the operation of the joint account with the *client*, another practice or another third party, *you* must:

(a) ensure that *you* receive the statements or duplicate statements from the *bank*, *building society* or other financial institution in accordance with rule 29.11, and retain them in accordance with rule 29.17(b)(ii); and

(b) ensure that *you* either have possession of any passbooks, or take copies of the passbook entries before handing any passbook to the other signatory, and retain them in accordance with rule 29.17(b)(ii).

Operation of the joint account by the other account holder

9.4   If the joint account is operated solely by the other account holder, *you* must ensure that *you* receive the statements or duplicate statements from the *bank*, *building society* or other financial institution in accordance with rule 29.11, and retain them in accordance with rule 29.17(b)(ii).

Rule 10: Operation of a client's own account

10.1   If, in the course of practice, *you* operate a *client's* own account as signatory (for example, as donee under a power of attorney), the rules in general do not apply, but the following must be complied with:

(a) rule 30.1 to 30.4 – accounting records for clients' own accounts;

(b) rule 31 – production of records; and

(c) rule 39.1(n) and (p) – reporting accountant to check compliance.

Operation by you only

10.2   If the account is operated by *you* only, *you* must ensure that *you* receive the statements from the *bank*, *building society* or other financial institution in accordance with rule 30, and have possession of any passbooks.

Shared operation of the account

10.3   If *you* share the operation of the account with the *client* or a co-attorney outside *your firm*, *you* must:

(a) ensure that *you* receive the statements or duplicate statements from the *bank*, *building society* or other financial institution and retain them in accordance with rule 30.1 to 30.4; and

(b) ensure that *you* either have possession of any passbooks, or take copies of the passbook entries before handing any passbook to the *client* or co-attorney, and retain them in accordance with rule 30.1 to 30.4.

Operation of the account for a limited purpose

10.4   If *you* are given authority (whether as attorney or otherwise) to operate the account for a limited purpose only, such as the taking up of a share rights issue during the *client's* temporary absence, *you* need not receive statements or possess passbooks, provided that *you* retain details of all cheques drawn or paid in, and retain copies of all passbook entries, relating to the transaction, and retain them in accordance with rule 30.1 to 30.3.

Application

10.5   This rule applies only to private practice. It does not cover money held or received by a donee of a power of attorney acting in a purely personal capacity outside any legal practice (see rule 4, guidance notes (iii)–(iv)).

10.6   A *"client's* own account" covers all accounts in a *client's* own name, whether opened by the *client* himself or herself, or by *you* on the *client's* instructions under rule 15.1(b). A *"client's* own account" also includes an account opened in the name of a person designated by the *client* under rule 15.1(b).

Guidance notes

(i)   Money held in a client's own account (under a power of attorney or otherwise) is not "client money" for the purpose of the rules because it is not "held or received" by you. If you close the account and receive the closing balance, this becomes client money subject to all the rules.

(ii)   Merely paying money into a client's own account, or helping the client to complete forms in relation to such an account, is not "operating" the account.

(iii)   If as executor you operate the deceased's account (whether before or after the grant of probate), you will be subject to the limited requirements of rule 10. If the account is subsequently transferred into your name, or a new account is opened in your name, you will have "held or received" client money and are then subject to all the rules.

Rule 11: Firm's rights not affected

11.1   Nothing in these rules deprives *you* of any recourse or right, whether by way of lien, set off, counterclaim, charge or otherwise, against money standing to the credit of a *client account*.

Rule 12: Categories of money

12.1   These rules do not apply to *out-of-scope money*, save to the limited extent specified in the rules. All other money held or received in the course of practice falls into one or other of the following categories:

(a)   "client money" – money held or received for a *client* or as *trustee*, and all other money which is not *office money*; or

(b)   "office money" – money which belongs to *you* or *your firm*.

12.2   "Client money" includes money held or received:

(a)   as *trustee*;

(b) as agent, bailee, stakeholder, or as the donee of a power of attorney, or as a liquidator, trustee in bankruptcy, *Court of Protection deputy* or trustee of an occupational pension scheme;

(c) for payment of unpaid *professional disbursements*;

(d) for payment of stamp duty land tax, Land Registry registration fees, telegraphic transfer fees and court fees (but see also guidance note (i));

(e) as a payment on account of *costs* generally;

(f) as a financial benefit paid in respect of a *client*, unless the *client* has given *you* prior authority to retain it (see Chapter 1, outcome 1.15 and indicative behaviour 1.20 of the *SRA Code of Conduct*);

(g) jointly with another person outside the *firm*.

12.3   Money held to the sender's order is *client money*.

(a) If money is accepted on such terms, it must be held in a *client account*.

(b) However, a cheque or draft sent to *you* on terms that the cheque or draft (as opposed to the money) is held to the sender's order must not be presented for payment without the sender's consent.

(c) The recipient is always subject to a professional obligation to return the money, or the cheque or draft, to the sender on demand.

12.4   An advance to a *client* which is paid into a *client account* under rule 14.2(b) becomes *client money*.

12.5   A cheque in respect of damages and *costs*, made payable to the *client* but paid into a *client account* under rule 14.2(e), becomes *client money*.

12.6   Endorsing a cheque or draft over to a *client* or employer in the course of practice amounts to receiving *client money*. Even if no other *client money* is held or received, *you* must comply with some provisions of the rules, e.g.:

(a) rule 7 (duty to remedy breaches);

(b) rule 29 (accounting records for client money);

(c) rule 31 (production of records);

(d) rule 32 (delivery of accountants' reports).

12.7   "Office money" includes:

(a) money held or received in connection with running the *firm*; for example, PAYE, or VAT on the *firm's fees*;

(b) *interest* on *general client accounts*; the *bank* or *building society* should be instructed to credit such *interest* to the *office account* – but see also rule 14.2(d); and

(c) payments received in respect of:

    (i) *fees* due to the *firm* against a bill or written notification of *costs* incurred, which has been given or sent in accordance with rule 17.2;

    (ii) *disbursements* already paid by the *firm*;

    (iii) *disbursements* incurred but not yet paid by the *firm*, but excluding unpaid *professional disbursements*;

    (iv) money paid for or towards an *agreed fee*; and

(d) money held in a *client account* and earmarked for *costs* under rule 17.3; and

(e) money held or received from the Legal Services Commission as a *regular payment* (see rule 19.2).

12.8   If a *firm* conducts a personal or office transaction – for instance, conveyancing – for a *principal* (or for a number of *principals*), money held or received on behalf of the *principal(s)* is *office money*. However, other circumstances may mean that the money is *client money*, for example:

(a) If the *firm* also acts for a lender, money held or received on behalf of the lender is *client money*.

(b) If the *firm* acts for a *principal* and, for example, his or her spouse jointly (assuming the spouse is not a *partner* in the practice), money received on their joint behalf is *client money*.

(c) If the *firm* acts for an assistant *solicitor*, consultant or non-solicitor employee, or (if it is a *company*) a *director*, or (if it is an *LLP*) a member, he or she is regarded as a *client* of the *firm*, and money received for him or her is *client money* – even if he or she conducts the matter personally.

Guidance notes

(i)   Money held or received for payment of stamp duty land tax, Land Registry registration fees, telegraphic transfer fees and court fees is not office money because you have not incurred an obligation to HMRC, the Land Registry, the bank or the court to pay the duty or fee; (on the other hand, if you have already paid the duty or fee out of your own resources, or have received the service on credit, or the bank's charge for a telegraphic transfer forms part of your profit costs, payment subsequently received from the client will be office money);

(ii)   Money held:

(a) by liquidators, trustees in bankruptcy, Court of Protection deputies and trustees of occupational pension schemes;

(b) jointly with another person outside the practice (for example, with a lay trustee, or with another firm);

is client money, subject to a limited application of the rules – see rules 8 and 9. The donee of a power of attorney, who operates the donor's own account, is also subject to a limited application of the rules (see rule 10), although money kept in the donor's own account is not "client money" because it is not "held or received" by the donee.

(iii)   If the SRA intervenes in a practice, money from the practice is held or received by the SRA's intervention agent subject to a trust under Schedule 1 paragraph 7(1) of the Solicitors Act 1974, and is therefore client money. The same provision requires the agent to pay the money into a client account.

(iv)   Money held or received in the course of employment when practising in one of the capacities listed in rule 5 (persons exempt from the rules) is not "client money" for the purpose of the rules, because the rules do not apply at all.

(v)   The receipt of out-of-scope money of an MDP which is mixed with other types of money is dealt with in rules 17 and 18.

(vi)   See Appendices 1 and 2 (which do not form part of the rules) for a summary of the effect of the rules and the treatment of different types of money.

PART 2: CLIENT MONEY AND OPERATION OF A CLIENT ACCOUNT

Rule 13: Client accounts

13.1   If *you* hold or receive *client money*, *you* must keep one or more *client accounts* (unless all the *client money* is always dealt with outside any *client account* in accordance with rule 8, rule 9, rule 15 or rule 16).

13.2   A "client account" is an account of a practice kept at a *bank* or *building society* for holding *client money*, in accordance with the requirements of this part of the rules.

13.3   The *client account(s)* of:

   (a)   a *sole practitioner* must be in the name under which the *sole practitioner* is recognised by the *SRA*, whether that is the *sole practitioner's* own name or the *firm* name;

   (b)   a *partnership* must be in the name under which the *partnership* is recognised by the *SRA*;

   (c)   an incorporated practice must be in the company name, or the name of the *LLP*, as registered at Companies House;

   (d)   in-house *solicitors* or *RELs* must be in the name of the current *principal solicitor/REL* or *solicitors/RELs*;

   (e)   *trustees*, where all the *trustees* of a *trust* are *managers* and/or employees of the same *recognised body* or *licensed body*, must be either in the name of the *recognised body/licensed body* or in the name of the *trustee(s)*;

   (f)   *trustees*, where all the *trustees* of a *trust* are the *sole practitioner* and/or his or her employees, must be either in the name under which the *sole practitioner* is recognised by the *SRA* or in the name of the *trustee(s)*;

and the name of the account must also include the word "client" in full (an abbreviation is not acceptable).

13.4 A *client account* must be:

(a) a *bank* account at a branch (or a *bank's* head office) in England and Wales; or

(b) a *building society* account at a branch (or a society's head office) in England and Wales.

13.5 There are two types of *client account*:

(a) a "separate designated client account", which is an account for money relating to a single *client*, other person or *trust*, and which includes in its title, in addition to the requirements of rule 13.3 above, a reference to the identity of the *client*, other person or *trust*; and

(b) a "general client account", which is any other *client account*.

13.6 Before opening a *client account*, a *licensed body* must enter into a written agreement with the *bank* or *building society* acknowledging that the account will hold *client money*, and that the *bank* or *building society* shall not have any recourse or right against the money standing to its credit in respect of any liability of the *licensed body* to the *bank* or *building society*, other than a liability in connection with the account. This requirement must also be complied with by a *firm* which becomes a *licensed body*, whether opening new *client accounts* or using its existing *client accounts*. The *licensed body* must ensure that the agreement is kept on foot.

13.7 The *clients* of a *licensed body* must be informed at the outset of the retainer, or during the course of the retainer as appropriate, if the *licensed body* is (or becomes) owned by a *bank* or *building society* and its *client account* is held at that *bank* or *building society* (or another *bank* or *building society* in the same group).

13.8 Money held in a *client account* must be immediately available, even at the sacrifice of *interest*, unless the *client* otherwise instructs, or the circumstances clearly indicate otherwise.

Guidance notes

(i) In the case of in-house practice, any client account should include the names of all solicitors or registered European lawyers held out on the notepaper as principals. The names of other employees who are solicitors or registered European lawyers may also be included if so desired. Any person whose name is included will have to be included on the accountant's report.

(ii) A firm may have any number of separate designated client accounts and general client accounts.

(iii) Compliance with rule 13.1 to 13.4 ensures that clients of a recognised body or recognised sole practitioner, as well as the bank or building society, have the protection afforded by section 85 of the Solicitors Act 1974. Rule 13.6 seeks to give protection, similar to that afforded by section 85, to clients of licensed bodies. It will be repealed on the coming into force of the Order referred to in rule 53 which will give the equivalent statutory protections to client money held by a licensed body.

Rule 14: Use of a client account

14.1 *Client money* must *without delay* be paid into a *client account*, and must be held in a *client account*, except when the rules provide to the contrary (see rules 8, 9, 15, 16, 17 and 19).

14.2 Only *client money* may be paid into or held in a *client account*, except:

(a) an amount of the *firm's* own money required to open or maintain the account;

(b) an advance from the *firm* to fund a payment on behalf of a *client* or *trust* in excess of funds held for that *client* or *trust*; the sum becomes *client money* on payment into the account (for *interest* on *client money*, see rule 22.2(c));

(c) money to replace any sum which for any reason has been drawn from the account in breach of rule 20; the replacement money becomes *client money* on payment into the account;

(d) *interest* which is paid into a *client account* to enable payment from the *client account* of all money owed to the *client*; and

(e) a cheque in respect of damages and *costs*, made payable to the *client*, which is paid into the *client account* pursuant to the *Society's* Conditional Fee Agreement; the sum becomes *client money* on payment into the account (but see rule 17.1(e) for the transfer of the *costs* element from *client account*);

and except when the rules provide to the contrary (see guidance note (ii) below).

14.3 *Client money* must be returned to the *client* (or other person on whose behalf the money is held) promptly, as soon as there is no longer any proper reason to retain those funds. Payments received after *you* have already accounted to the *client*, for example by way of a refund, must be paid to the *client* promptly.

14.4 *You* must promptly inform a *client* (or other person on whose behalf the money is held) in writing of the amount of any *client money* retained at the end of a matter (or the substantial conclusion of a matter), and the reason for that retention. *You* must inform the *client* (or other person) in writing at least once every twelve months thereafter of the amount of *client money* still held and the reason for the retention, for as long as *you* continue to hold that money.

14.5 *You* must not provide banking facilities through a *client account*. Payments into, and transfers or withdrawals from, a *client account* must be in respect of instructions relating to an underlying transaction (and the funds arising therefrom) or to a service forming part of *your* normal regulated activities.

Guidance notes

(i)   Exceptions to rule 14.1 (client money must be paid into a client account) can be found in:

(a)   rule 8 – liquidators, trustees in bankruptcy, Court of Protection deputies and trustees of occupational pension schemes;

(b)   rule 9 – joint accounts;

(c)   rule 15 – client's instructions;

(d)   rule 16 – cash paid straight to client, beneficiary or third party;

    (A)   cheque endorsed to client, beneficiary or third party;

    (B)   money withheld from client account on the SRA's authority;

    (C)   money withheld from client account in accordance with a trustee's powers;

(e)   rule 17.1(b) – receipt and transfer of costs;

(f)   rule 19.1 – payments by the Legal Services Commission.

(ii)   Rule 14.2(a) to (d) provides for exceptions to the principle that only client money may be paid into a client account. Additional exceptions can be found in:

(a)   rule 17.1(c) – receipt and transfer of costs;

(b)   rule 18.2(b) – receipt of mixed payments;

(c)   rule 19.2(c)(ii) – transfer to client account of a sum for unpaid professional disbursements, where regular payments are received from the Legal Services Commission.

(iii)   Only a nominal sum will be required to open or maintain an account. In practice, banks will usually open (and, if instructed, keep open) accounts with nil balances.

(iv)   If client money is invested in the purchase of assets other than money – such as stocks or shares – it ceases to be client money, because it is no longer money held by the firm. If the investment is subsequently sold, the money received is, again, client money. The records kept under rule 29 will need to include entries to show the purchase or sale of investments.

(v)   Rule 14.5 reflects decisions of the Solicitors Disciplinary Tribunal that it is not a proper part of a solicitor's everyday business or practice to operate a banking facility for third parties, whether they are clients of the firm or not. It should be noted that any exemption under the Financial Services and Markets Act 2000 is likely to be lost if a deposit is taken in circumstances which do not form part of your practice. It should also be borne in mind that there are criminal sanctions against assisting money launderers.

(vi)   As with rule 7 (Duty to remedy breaches), "promptly" in rule 14.3 and 14.4 is not defined but should be given its natural meaning in the particular circumstances. Accounting to a client for any surplus funds will often fall naturally at the end of a matter. Other retainers may be more protracted and, even when the principal work has been completed, funds may still be needed, for example, to cover outstanding work in a conveyancing transaction or to meet a tax liability. (See also paragraphs 4.8 and 4.9 of the Guidelines for accounting procedures and systems at Appendix 3.)

(vii)   There may be some instances when, during the course of a retainer, the specific purpose for which particular funds were paid no longer exists, for example, the need to instruct counsel or a medical expert. Rule 14.3 is concerned with returning funds to clients at the end of a matter (or the substantial conclusion of a matter) and is not intended to apply to ongoing retainers. However, in order to act in the best interests of your client, you may need to take instructions in such circumstances to ascertain, for instance, whether the money should be returned to the client or retained to cover the general funding or other aspects of the case.

(viii)   See rule 20.1(j)–(k) for withdrawals from a client account when the rightful owner of funds cannot be traced. The obligation to report regularly under rule 14.4 ceases to apply if you are no longer able to trace the client, at which point rule 20.1(j) or (k) would apply.

Rule 15: Client money withheld from client account on client's instructions

15.1   *Client money* may be:

(a)   held by *you* outside a *client account* by, for example, retaining it in the *firm's* safe in the form of cash, or placing it in an account in the *firm's* name which is not a *client account*, such as an account outside England and Wales; or

(b)   paid into an account at a *bank*, *building society* or other financial institution opened in the name of the *client* or of a person designated by the *client*;

but only if the *client* instructs *you* to that effect for the *client's* own convenience, and only if the instructions are given in writing, or are given by other means and confirmed by *you* to the *client* in writing.

15.2   It is improper to seek blanket agreements, through standard terms of business or otherwise, to hold *client money* outside a *client account*.

15.3   If a *client* instructs *you* to hold part only of a payment in accordance with rule 15.1(a) or (b), the entire payment must first be placed in a *client account*, before transferring the relevant part out and dealing with it in accordance with the *client's* instructions.

15.4   A payment on account of *costs* received from a person who is funding all or part of *your fees* may be withheld from a *client account* on the instructions of that person given in accordance with rule 15.1.

Guidance notes

(i)   Money withheld from a client account under rule 15.1(a) remains client money, and all the record-keeping provisions of rule 29 will apply.

(ii)   Once money has been paid into an account set up under rule 15.1(b), it ceases to be client money. Until that time, the money is client money and, under rule 29, a record is required of your receipt of the money, and its payment into the account in the name of the client or designated person. If you can operate the account, rule 10 (operating a client's own account) and rule 30 (accounting records for clients' own accounts) will apply. In the absence of instructions to the contrary, rule 14.1 requires any money withdrawn to be paid into a client account.

(iii)   Rule 29.17(d) requires clients' instructions under rule 15.1 to be kept for at least six years.

Rule 16: Other client money withheld from a client account

16.1   The following categories of *client money* may be withheld from a *client account*:

(a)   cash received and *without delay* paid in cash in the ordinary course of business to the *client* or, on the *client's* behalf, to a third party, or paid in cash in the execution of a *trust* to a beneficiary or third party;

(b)   a cheque or draft received and endorsed over in the ordinary course of business to the *client* or, on the *client's* behalf, to a third party, or *without delay* endorsed over in the execution of a *trust* to a beneficiary or third party;

(c)   money withheld from a *client account* on instructions under rule 15;

(d)   money which, in accordance with a *trustee's* powers, is paid into or retained in an account of the *trustee* which is not a *client account* (for example, an account outside England and Wales), or properly retained in cash in the performance of the *trustee's* duties;

(e)   unpaid *professional disbursements* included in a payment of *costs* dealt with under rule 17.1(b);

(f)   in respect of payments from the Legal Services Commission:

(i)   advance payments from the Legal Services Commission withheld from *client account* (see rule 19.1(a)); and

(ii)   unpaid *professional disbursements* included in a payment of *costs* from the Legal Services Commission (see rule 19.1(b)); and

(g)   money withheld from a *client account* on the written authorisation of the

SRA. The *SRA* may impose a condition that the money is paid to a charity which gives an indemnity against any legitimate claim subsequently made for the sum received.

Guidance notes

(i) If money is withheld from a client account under rule 16.1(a) or (b), rule 29 requires records to be kept of the receipt of the money and the payment out.

(ii) If money is withheld from a client account under rule 16.1(d), rule 29 requires a record to be kept of the receipt of the money, and requires the inclusion of the money in the monthly reconciliations. (Money held by a trustee jointly with another party is subject only to the limited requirements of rule 9.)

(iii) It makes no difference, for the purpose of the rules, whether an endorsement is effected by signature in the normal way or by some other arrangement with the bank.

(iv) The circumstances in which authorisation would be given under rule 16.1(g) must be extremely rare. Applications for authorisation should be made to the Professional Ethics Guidance Team.

Rule 17: Receipt and transfer of costs

17.1 When *you* receive money paid in full or part settlement of *your* bill (or other notification of *costs*) *you* **must follow one of the following five options:**

(a) **determine the composition of the payment without delay, and deal with the money accordingly:**

    (i) if the sum comprises *office money* and/or *out-of-scope money* only, it must be placed in an *office account*;

    (ii) if the sum comprises only *client money*, the entire sum must be placed in a *client account*;

    (iii) if the sum includes both *office money* and *client money*, or *client money* and *out-of-scope money*, or *client money, out-of-scope money* and *office money*, *you* must follow rule 18 (receipt of mixed payments); or

(b) **ascertain that the payment comprises only *office money* and/or *out-of-scope money*, and/or *client money* in the form of *professional disbursements* incurred but not yet paid, and deal with the payment as follows:**

    (i) place the entire sum in an *office account* at a *bank* or *building society* branch (or head office) in England and Wales; and

    (ii) by the end of the second working day following receipt, either pay any unpaid *professional disbursement*, or transfer a sum for its settlement to a *client account*; **or**

(c) **pay the entire sum into a *client account* (regardless of its composition), and** transfer any *office money* and/or *out-of-scope money* out of the *client account* within 14 days of receipt; or

(d) on receipt of *costs* from the Legal Services Commission, follow the option in rule 19.1(b); or

(e) in relation to a cheque paid into a *client account* under rule 14.2(e), transfer the *costs* element out of the *client account* within 14 days of receipt.

17.2 If *you* properly require payment of *your fees* from money held for a *client* or *trust* in a *client account*, *you* must first give or send a bill of *costs*, or other written notification of the *costs* incurred, to the *client* or the paying party.

17.3 Once *you* have complied with rule 17.2 above, the money earmarked for *costs* becomes *office money* and must be transferred out of the *client account* within 14 days.

17.4 A payment on account of *costs* generally in respect of those activities for which the practice is regulated by the *SRA* is *client money*, and must be held in a *client account* until *you* have complied with rule 17.2 above. (For an exception in the case of legal aid payments, see rule 19.1(a). See also rule 18 on dealing with mixed payments of *client money* and/or *out-of-scope money* when part of a payment on account of *costs* relates to activities not regulated by the *SRA*.)

17.5 A payment for an *agreed fee* must be paid into an *office account*. An "agreed fee" is one that is fixed – not a *fee* that can be varied upwards, nor a *fee* that is dependent on the transaction being completed. An *agreed fee* must be evidenced in writing.

17.6 *You* will not be in breach of rule 17 as a result of a misdirected electronic payment or other direct transfer from a *client* or paying third party, provided:

(a) appropriate systems are in place to ensure compliance;

(b) appropriate instructions were given to the *client* or paying third party;

(c) the *client's* or paying third party's mistake is remedied promptly upon discovery; and

(d) appropriate steps are taken to avoid future errors by the *client* or paying third party.

17.7 *Costs* transferred out of a *client account* in accordance with rule 17.2 and 17.3 must be specific sums relating to the bill or other written notification of *costs*, and covered by the amount held for the particular *client* or *trust*. Round sum withdrawals on account of *costs* are a breach of the rules.

17.8 In the case of a *trust* of which the only *trustee(s)* are within the *firm*, the paying party will be the *trustee(s)* themselves. *You* must keep the original bill or notification of *costs* on the file, in addition to complying with rule 29.15 (central record or file of copy bills, etc.).

17.9   Undrawn *costs* must not remain in a *client account* as a "cushion" against any future errors which could result in a shortage on that account, and cannot be regarded as available to set off against any general shortage on *client account*.

Guidance notes

(i)   This note lists types of disbursement and how they are categorised:

    (a)   Money received for paid disbursements is office money.

    (b)   Money received for unpaid professional disbursements is client money.

    (c)   Money received for other unpaid disbursements for which you have incurred a liability to the payee (for example, travel agents' charges, taxi fares, courier charges or Land Registry search fees, payable on credit) is office money.

    (d)   Money received for disbursements anticipated but not yet incurred is a payment on account, and is therefore client money.

(ii)   The option in rule 17.1(a) allows you to place all payments in the correct account in the first instance. The option in rule 17.1(b) allows the prompt banking into an office account of an invoice payment when the only uncertainty is whether or not the payment includes some client money in the form of unpaid professional disbursements. The option in rule 17.1(c) allows the prompt banking into a client account of any invoice payment in advance of determining whether the payment is a mixture of office and client money (of whatever description), or client money and out-of-scope money, or client money, out-of-scope money and office money, or is only office money and/or out-of-scope money.

(iii)   If you are not in a position to comply with the requirements of rule 17.1(b), you cannot take advantage of that option.

(iv)   The option in rule 17.1(b) cannot be used if the money received includes a payment on account – for example, a payment for a professional disbursement anticipated but not yet incurred.

(v)   In order to be able to use the option in rule 17.1(b) for electronic payments or other direct transfers from clients, you may choose to establish a system whereby clients are given an office account number for payment of costs. The system must be capable of ensuring that, when invoices are sent to the client, no request is made for any client money, with the sole exception of money for professional disbursements already incurred but not yet paid.

(vi)   Rule 17.1(c) allows clients to be given a single account number for making direct payments by electronic or other means – under this option, it has to be a client account.

(vii)   "Properly" in rule 17.2 implies that the work has actually been done, whether at the end of the matter or at an interim stage, and that you are entitled to appropriate the money for costs. For example, the costs set out in a completion statement in a conveyancing transaction will become due on completion and should be transferred out of the client account within 14 days of completion in accordance with rule 17.3. The requirement to transfer costs out of the client account within a set time is intended to prevent costs being left on client account to conceal a shortage.

(viii) Money is "earmarked" for costs under rule 17.2 and 17.3 when you decide to use funds already held in client account to settle your bill. If you wish to obtain the client's prior approval, you will need to agree the amount to be taken with your client before issuing the bill to avoid the possibility of failing to meet the 14 day time limit for making the transfer out of client account. If you wish to retain the funds, for example, as money on account of costs on another matter, you will need to ask the client to send the full amount in settlement of the bill. If, when submitting a bill, you fail to indicate whether you intend to take your costs from client account, or expect the client to make a payment, you will be regarded as having "earmarked" your costs.

(ix) An amendment to section 69 of the Solicitors Act 1974 by the Legal Services Act 2007 permits a solicitor or recognised body to sue on a bill which has been signed electronically and which the client has agreed can be delivered electronically.

(x) The rules do not require a bill of costs for an agreed fee, although your VAT position may mean that in practice a bill is needed. If there is no bill, the written evidence of the agreement must be filed as a written notification of costs under rule 29.15(b).

(xi) The bill of an MDP may be in respect of costs for work of the SRA-regulated part of the practice, and also for work that falls outside the scope of SRA regulation. Money received in respect of the non-SRA regulated work, including money for disbursements, is out-of-scope money and must be dealt with in accordance with rule 17.

(xii) See Chapter 1, indicative behaviour 1.21 of the SRA Code of Conduct in relation to ensuring that disbursements included in a bill reflect the actual amount spent or to be spent.

Rule 18: Receipt of mixed payments

18.1 A "mixed payment" is one which includes *client money* as well as *office money* and/or *out-of-scope money*.

18.2 A *mixed payment* must either:

(a) be split between a *client account* and *office account* as appropriate; or

(b) be placed *without delay* in a *client account*.

18.3 If the entire payment is placed in a *client account*, all *office money* and/or *out-of-scope money* must be transferred out of the *client account* within 14 days of receipt.

> ### Guidance notes
>
> (i) See rule 17.1(b) and (c) for additional ways of dealing with (among other things) mixed payments received in response to a bill or other notification of costs.
>
> (ii) See rule 19.1(b) for (among other things) mixed payments received from the Legal Services Commission.
>
> (iii) Some out-of-scope money may be subject to the rules of other regulators which may require an earlier withdrawal from the client account operated under these rules.

Rule 19: Treatment of payments to legal aid practitioners

Payments from the Legal Services Commission

19.1 Two special dispensations apply to payments (other than *regular payments*) from the Legal Services Commission:

(a) An advance payment, which may include *client money*, may be placed in an *office account*, provided the Commission instructs in writing that this may be done.

(b) A payment for *costs* (interim and/or final) may be paid into an *office account* at a *bank* or *building society* branch (or head office) in England and Wales, regardless of whether it consists wholly of *office money*, or is mixed with *client money* in the form of:

(i) advance payments for *fees* or *disbursements*; or

(ii) money for unpaid *professional disbursements*;

provided all money for payment of *disbursements* is transferred to a *client account* (or the *disbursements* paid) within 14 days of receipt.

19.2 The following provisions apply to *regular payments* from the Legal Services Commission:

(a) "Regular payments" (which are *office money*) are:

(i) standard monthly payments paid by the Commission under the civil legal aid contracting arrangements;

(ii) standard monthly payments paid by the Commission under the criminal legal aid contracting arrangements; and

(iii) any other payments for work done or to be done received from the Commission under an arrangement for payments on a regular basis.

(b) *Regular payments* must be paid into an *office account* at a *bank* or *building society* branch (or head office) in England and Wales.

(c) *You* must within 28 days of submitting a report to the Commission, notifying completion of a matter, either:

    (i) pay any unpaid *professional disbursement(s)*, or

    (ii) transfer to a *client account* a sum equivalent to the amount of any unpaid *professional disbursement(s)*,

relating to that matter.

(d) In cases where the Commission permits *you* to submit reports at various stages during a matter rather than only at the end of a matter, the requirement in rule 19.2(c) above applies to any unpaid *professional disbursement(s)* included in each report so submitted.

Payments from a third party

19.3 If the Legal Services Commission has paid any *costs* to *you* or a previously nominated *firm* in a matter (advice and assistance or legal help *costs*, advance payments or interim *costs*), or has paid *professional disbursements* direct, and *costs* are subsequently settled by a third party:

(a) The entire third party payment must be paid into a *client account*.

(b) A sum representing the payments made by the Commission must be retained in the *client account*.

(c) Any balance belonging to *you* must be transferred to an *office account* within 14 days of *your* sending a report to the Commission containing details of the third party payment.

(d) The sum retained in the *client account* as representing payments made by the Commission must be:

    (i) **either** recorded in the individual *client's* ledger account, and identified as the Commission's money;

    (ii) **or** recorded in a ledger account in the Commission's name, and identified by reference to the *client* or matter;

and kept in the *client account* until notification from the Commission that it has recouped an equivalent sum from subsequent payments due to *you*. The retained sum must be transferred to an *office account* within 14 days of notification.

19.4 Any part of a third party payment relating to unpaid *professional disbursements* or outstanding *costs* of the *client's* previous *firm* is *client money*, and must be kept in a *client account* until *you* pay the *professional disbursement* or outstanding *costs*.

Guidance notes

(i)   This rule deals with matters which specifically affect legal aid practitioners. It should not be read in isolation from the remainder of the rules which apply to everyone, including legal aid practitioners.

(ii)   In cases carried out under public funding certificates, firms can apply for advance payments ("Payments on Account" under the Standard Civil Contract). The Legal Services Commission has agreed that these payments may be placed in office account.

(iii)   Rule 19.1(b) deals with the specific problems of legal aid practitioners by allowing a mixed or indeterminate payment of costs (or even a payment consisting entirely of unpaid professional disbursements) to be paid into an office account, which for the purpose of rule 19.1(b) must be an account at a bank or building society. However, it is always open to you to comply with rule 17.1(a) to (c), which are the options for everyone for the receipt of costs. For regular payments, see guidance notes (v)–(vii) below.

(iv)   Firms are required by the Legal Services Commission to report promptly to the Commission on receipt of costs from a third party. It is advisable to keep a copy of the report on the file as proof of compliance with the Commission's requirements, as well as to demonstrate compliance with the rule.

(v)   Rule 19.2(c) permits a firm, which is required to transfer an amount to cover unpaid professional disbursements into a client account, to make the transfer from its own resources if the regular payments are insufficient.

(vi)   The 28 day time limit for paying, or transferring an amount to a client account for, unpaid professional disbursements is for the purposes of these rules only. An earlier deadline may be imposed by contract with the Commission or with counsel, agents or experts. On the other hand, you may have agreed to pay later than 28 days from the submission of the report notifying completion of a matter, in which case rule 19.2(c) will require a transfer of the appropriate amount to a client account (but not payment) within 28 days.

(vii)   For the appropriate accounting records for regular payments, see rule 29.7.

Rule 20: Withdrawals from a client account

20.1   *Client money* may only be withdrawn from a *client account* when it is:

   (a)   properly required for a payment to or on behalf of the *client* (or other person on whose behalf the money is being held);

   (b)   properly required for a payment in the execution of a particular *trust*, including the purchase of an investment (other than money) in accordance with the *trustee's* powers;

(c) properly required for payment of a *disbursement* on behalf of the *client* or *trust*;

(d) properly required in full or partial reimbursement of money spent by *you* on behalf of the *client* or *trust*;

(e) transferred to another *client account*;

(f) withdrawn on the *client's* instructions, provided the instructions are for the *client's* convenience and are given in writing, or are given by other means and confirmed by *you* to the *client* in writing;

(g) transferred to an account other than a *client account* (such as an account outside England and Wales), or retained in cash, by a *trustee* in the proper performance of his or her duties;

(h) a refund to *you* of an advance no longer required to fund a payment on behalf of a *client* or *trust* (see rule 14.2(b));

(i) money which has been paid into the account in breach of the rules (for example, money paid into the wrong *separate designated client account*) – see rule 20.5 below;

(j) money not covered by (a) to (i) above, where *you* comply with the conditions set out in rule 20.2; or

(k) money not covered by (a) to (i) above, withdrawn from the account on the written authorisation of the *SRA*. The *SRA* may impose a condition that *you* pay the money to a charity which gives an indemnity against any legitimate claim subsequently made for the sum received.

20.2   A withdrawal of *client money* under rule 20.1(j) above may be made only where the amount held does not exceed £50 in relation to any one individual *client* or *trust* matter and *you*:

(a) establish the identity of the owner of the money, or make reasonable attempts to do so;

(b) make adequate attempts to ascertain the proper destination of the money, and to return it to the rightful owner, unless the reasonable costs of doing so are likely to be excessive in relation to the amount held;

(c) pay the funds to a charity;

(d) record the steps taken in accordance with rule 20.2(a)–(c) above and retain those records, together with all relevant documentation (including receipts from the charity), in accordance with rule 29.16 and 29.17(a); and

(e) keep a central register in accordance with rule 29.22.

20.3   *Office money* may only be withdrawn from a *client account* when it is:

(a) money properly paid into the account to open or maintain it under rule 14.2(a);

(b) properly required for payment of *your costs* under rule 17.2 and 17.3;

(c) the whole or part of a payment into a *client account* under rule 17.1(c);

(d) part of a *mixed payment* placed in a *client account* under rule 18.2(b); or

(e) money which has been paid into a *client account* in breach of the rules (for example, *interest* wrongly credited to a *general client account*) – see rule 20.5 below.

20.4   *Out-of-scope money* must be withdrawn from a *client account* in accordance with rules 17.1(a), 17.1(c) and 18 as appropriate.

20.5   Money which has been paid into a *client account* in breach of the rules must be withdrawn from the *client account* promptly upon discovery.

20.6   Money withdrawn in relation to a particular *client* or *trust* from a *general client account* must not exceed the money held on behalf of that *client* or *trust* in all *your general client accounts* (except as provided in rule 20.7 below).

20.7   *You* may make a payment in respect of a particular *client* or *trust* out of a *general client account*, even if no money (or insufficient money) is held for that *client* or *trust* in *your general client account(s)*, provided:

(a) sufficient money is held for that *client* or *trust* in a *separate designated client account*; and

(b) the appropriate transfer from the *separate designated client account* to a *general client account* is made immediately.

20.8   Money held for a *client* or *trust* in a *separate designated client account* must not be used for payments for another *client* or *trust*.

20.9   A *client account* must not be overdrawn, except in the following circumstances:

(a) A *separate designated client account* operated in *your* capacity as *trustee* can be overdrawn if *you* make payments on behalf of the *trust* (for example, inheritance tax) before realising sufficient assets to cover the payments.

(b) If a *sole practitioner* dies and his or her *client accounts* are frozen, overdrawn *client accounts* can be operated in accordance with the rules to the extent of the money held in the frozen accounts.

Guidance notes

(i) Withdrawals in favour of firm, and for payment of disbursements

(a) Disbursements to be paid direct from a client account, or already paid out of your own money, can be withdrawn under rule 20.1(c) or (d) in advance of preparing a bill of costs. Money to be withdrawn from a client account for the payment of costs (fees and disbursements) under rule 17.2 and 17.3 becomes office money and is dealt with under rule 20.3(b).

(b) Money is "spent" under rule 20.1(d) at the time when you despatch a cheque, unless the cheque is to be held to your order. Money is also regarded as "spent" by the use of a credit account, so that, for example, search fees, taxi fares and courier charges incurred in this way may be transferred to your office account.

(c) See rule 21.4 for the way in which a withdrawal from a client account in your favour must be effected.

(ii) Cheques payable to banks, building societies, etc.

(a) In order to protect client money against misappropriation when cheques are made payable to banks, building societies or other large institutions, it is strongly recommended that you add the name and number of the account after the payee's name.

(iii) Drawing against uncleared cheques

(a) You should use discretion in drawing against a cheque received from or on behalf of a client before it has been cleared. If the cheque is not met, other clients' money will have been used to make the payment in breach of the rules (see rule 7 (duty to remedy breaches)). You may be able to avoid a breach of the rules by instructing the bank or building society to charge all unpaid credits to your office or personal account.

(iv) Non-receipt of electronic payments

(a) If you withdraw money from a general client account on the strength of information that an electronic payment is on its way, but the electronic payment does not arrive, you will have used other clients' money in breach of the rules. See also rule 7 (duty to remedy breaches).

(v) Withdrawals on instructions

(a) One of the reasons why a client might authorise a withdrawal under rule 20.1(f) might be to have the money transferred to a type of account other than a client account. If so, the requirements of rule 15 must be complied with.

(vi) Withdrawals where the rightful owner cannot be traced, on the SRA's authorisation and without SRA authorisation

(a) Applications for authorisation under rule 20.1(k) should be made to the Professional Ethics Guidance Team, who can advise on the criteria which must normally be met for authorisation to be given. You may under rule 20.1(j) pay to a charity sums of £50 or less per client or trust matter without the SRA's authorisation, provided the safeguards set out in rule 20.2 are followed. You may, however, if you prefer, apply to the SRA for prior authorisation in all cases.

(b) You will need to apply to the SRA, whatever the amount involved, if the money to be withdrawn is not to be paid to a charity. This situation might arise, for example, if you have been unable to deliver a bill of costs because the client has become untraceable and so cannot make a transfer from client account to office account in accordance with rule 17.2–17.3.

(c) After a practice has been wound up, surplus balances are sometimes discovered in an old client account. This money remains subject to rule 20 and rule 21. An application can be made to the SRA under rule 20.1(k).

Rule 21: Method of and authority for withdrawals from client account

21.1   A withdrawal from a *client account* may be made only after a specific authority in respect of that withdrawal has been signed by an appropriate person or persons in accordance with the *firm's* procedures for signing on *client account*. An authority for withdrawals from *client account* may be signed electronically, subject to appropriate safeguards and controls.

21.2   *Firms* must put in place appropriate systems and procedures governing withdrawals from *client account*, including who should be permitted by the *firm* to sign on *client account*. A non-*manager* owner or a non-employee owner of a *licensed body* is not an appropriate person to be a signatory on *client account* and must not be permitted by the *firm* to act in this way.

21.3   There is no need to comply with rule 21.1 above when transferring money from one *general client account* to another *general client account* at the same *bank* or *building society*.

21.4   A withdrawal from a *client account* in *your* favour must be either by way of a cheque, or by way of a transfer to the *office account* or to *your* personal account. The withdrawal must not be made in cash.

Guidance notes

(i)   A firm should select suitable people to authorise withdrawals from the client account. Firms will wish to consider whether any employee should be able to sign on client account, and whether signing rights should be given to all managers of the practice or limited to those managers directly involved in providing legal services. Someone who has no day-to-day involvement in the business of the practice is unlikely to be regarded as a suitable signatory because of the lack of proximity to client matters. An appropriate understanding of the requirements of the rules is essential – see paragraph 4.2 of the Guidelines for accounting procedures and systems at Appendix 3.

(ii)   Instructions to the bank or building society to withdraw money from a client account (rule 21.1) may be given over the telephone, provided a specific authority has been signed in accordance with this rule before the instructions are given. It is of paramount importance that there are appropriate in-built safeguards, such as passwords, to give the greatest protection possible for client money. Suitable safeguards will also be needed for practices which operate a CHAPS terminal or other form of electronic instruction for payment.

(iii)   In the case of a withdrawal by cheque, the specific authority (rule 21.1) is usually a signature on the cheque itself. Signing a blank cheque is not a specific authority.

(iv)   A withdrawal from a client account by way of a private loan from one client to another can only be made if the provisions of rule 27.2 are complied with.

(v)   If, in your capacity as trustee, you instruct an outside administrator to run, or continue to run, on a day-to-day basis, the business or property portfolio of an estate or trust, you will not need to comply with rule 21.1, provided all cheques are retained in accordance with rule 29.18. (See also rule 29, guidance note (ii)(d).)

(vi)   You may set up a "direct debit" system of payment for Land Registry application fees on either the office account or a client account. If a direct debit payment is to be taken from a client account for the payment of Land Registry application fees, a signature, which complies with the firm's systems and procedures set up under rule 21, on the application for registration will constitute the specific authority required by rule 21.1. As with any other payment method, care must be taken to ensure that sufficient uncommitted funds are held in the client account for the particular client before signing the authority. You should also bear in mind that should the Land Registry take an incorrect amount in error from a firm's client account (for example, a duplicate payment), the firm will be in breach of the rules if other clients' money has been used as a result.

(vii)   If you fail to specify the correct Land Registry fee on the application for registration (either by specifying a lesser amount than that actually due, or failing to specify any fee at all), you will be in breach of rule 21.1 if the Land Registry takes a sum from your client account greater than that specified on the application, without a specific authority for the revised sum being in place as required by rule 21. In order that you can comply with the rules, the Land Registry will need to contact you before taking the revised amount, so that the necessary authority may be signed prior to the revised amount being taken.

(viii)   Where the Land Registry contacts you by telephone, and you wish to authorise an immediate payment by direct debit over the telephone, you will first need to check that there is sufficient money held in client account for the client and, if there is, that it is not committed to some other purpose.

(ix)   The specific authority required by rule 21.1 can be signed after the telephone call has ended but must be signed before the additional payment (or correct full payment) is taken by the Land Registry. It is advisable to sign the authority promptly and, in any event, on the same day as the telephone instruction is given to the Land Registry to take the additional (or correct full) amount. If you decide to fund any extra amount from the office account, the transfer of office money to the client account would need to be made, preferably on the same day but, in any event, before the direct debit is taken. Your internal procedures would need to make it clear how to deal with such situations; for example, who should be consulted before a direct debit for an amount other than that specified on the application can be authorised, and the mechanism for ensuring the new authority is signed by a person permitted by the firm to sign on client account.

(x) You may decide to set up a direct debit system of payment on the office account because, for example, you do not wish to allow the Land Registry to have access to the firm's client account. Provided you are in funds, a transfer from the client account to the office account may be made under rule 20.1(d) to reimburse you as soon as the direct debit has been taken.

(xi) Variable "direct debit" payments to the Land Registry, as described in guidance notes (vi)–(x) above, are not direct debits in the usual sense as each payment is authorised and confirmed individually. A traditional direct debit or standing order should not be set up on a client account because of the need for a specific authority for each withdrawal.

PART 3: INTEREST

Rule 22: When interest must be paid

22.1 When *you* hold money in a *client account* for a *client*, or for a person funding all or part of *your fees*, or for a *trust*, *you* must account to the *client* or that person or *trust* for *interest* when it is fair and reasonable to do so in all the circumstances. (This also applies if money should have been held in a *client account* but was not. It also applies to money held in an account in accordance with rule 15.1(a) (or which should have been held in such an account), or rule 16.1(d).)

22.2 *You* are not required to pay *interest*:

- (a) on money held for the payment of a *professional disbursement*, once counsel etc. has requested a delay in settlement;

- (b) on money held for the Legal Services Commission;

- (c) on an advance from *you* under rule 14.2(b) to fund a payment on behalf of the *client* or *trust* in excess of funds held for that *client* or *trust*; or

- (d) if there is an agreement to contract out of the provisions of this rule under rule 25.

22.3 *You* must have a written policy on the payment of *interest*, which seeks to provide a fair outcome. The terms of the policy must be drawn to the attention of the *client* at the outset of a retainer, unless it is inappropriate to do so in the circumstances.

Guidance notes

(i) Requirement to pay interest

    (a) Money is normally held for a client as a necessary, but incidental, part of the retainer, to facilitate the carrying out of the client's instructions. The main purpose of the rules is to keep that money safe and available for the purpose for which it was provided. The rules also seek to provide for the payment of a fair sum of interest, when appropriate, which is unlikely to be as high as that obtainable by the client depositing those funds.

(b) An outcomes-focused approach has been adopted in this area, allowing firms the flexibility to set their own interest policies in order to achieve a fair outcome for both the client and the firm.

(c) In addition to your obligation under rule 22.3, it is good practice to explain your interest arrangements to clients. These will usually be based on client money being held in an instant access account to facilitate a transaction. Clients are unlikely to receive as much interest as might have been obtained had they held and invested the money themselves. A failure to explain the firm's policy on interest may lead to unrealistic expectations and, possibly, a complaint to the Legal Ombudsman.

(d) The Legal Services Act 2007 has abolished the distinction in the Solicitors Act 1974 between interest earned on client money held in a general client account or a separate designated client account, and therefore interest earned on the latter type of account is to be accounted for like interest on any other client money on a "fair and reasonable" basis. In practice, a firm which wishes to retain any part of the interest earned on client money will need to hold that money in a general client account and continue to have interest paid to the office account (see rule 12.7(b)). The tax regime still requires banks to deduct tax at source from interest earned on separate designated client accounts based on the tax status of the individual clients, making it impracticable to retain any part of the interest earned on that type of account.

(e) Some firms may wish to apply a de minimis by reference to the amount held and period for which it was held, for example, providing that no interest is payable if the amount calculated on the balance held is £20 or less. Any de minimis will need to be set at a reasonable level and regularly reviewed in the light of current interest rates.

(f) It is likely to be appropriate for firms to account for all interest earned in some circumstances, for example, where substantial sums of money are held for lengthy periods of time.

(g) If sums of money are held in relation to separate matters for the same client, it is normally appropriate to treat the money relating to the different matters separately but there may be cases when the matters are so closely related that they ought to be considered together, for example, when you are acting for a client in connection with numerous debt collection matters. Similarly, it may be fair and reasonable in the circumstances to aggregate sums of money held intermittently during the course of acting for a client.

(h) There is no requirement to pay interest on money held on instructions under rule 15.1(a) in a manner which attracts no interest.

(i)   Accounts opened in the client's name under rule 15.1(b) (whether operated by you or not) are not subject to rule 22, as the money is not held by you. All interest earned belongs to the client. The same applies to any account in the client's own name operated by you as signatory under rule 10.

(ii)   Interest policy (rule 22.3)

(a)   It is important that your clients should be aware of the terms of your interest policy. This should normally be covered at the outset of a retainer, although it may be unnecessary where you have acted for the client previously. It is open to you and your client to agree that interest will be dealt with in a different way (see rule 25).

(iii)   Unpresented cheques

(a)   A client may fail to present a cheque to his or her bank for payment. Whether or not it is reasonable to recalculate the amount due will depend on all the circumstances of the case. A reasonable charge may be made for any extra work carried out if you are legally entitled to make such a charge.

(iv)   Liquidators, trustees in bankruptcy, Court of Protection deputies and trustees of occupational pension schemes

(a)   Under rule 8, Part 3 of the rules does not normally apply to liquidators, etc. You must comply with the appropriate statutory rules and regulations, and rule 8.3 and 8.4 as appropriate.

(v)   Joint accounts

(a)   Under rule 9, Part 3 of the rules does not apply to joint accounts. If you hold money jointly with a client, interest earned on the account will be for the benefit of the client unless otherwise agreed. If money is held jointly with another practice, the allocation of interest earned will depend on the agreement reached.

(vi)   Failure to pay interest

(a)   A client, including one of joint clients, or a person funding all or part of your fees, may complain to the Legal Ombudsman if he or she believes that interest was due and has not been paid, or that the amount paid was insufficient. It is advisable for the client (or other person) to try to resolve the matter with you before approaching the Legal Ombudsman.

(vii)   Role of the reporting accountant

(a)   Paragraph 2.8 of the Guidelines for accounting procedures and systems at Appendix 3 states the need for policies and systems in relation to the payment of interest.

(b)   The reporting accountant does not check for compliance with the interest provisions but has a duty under rule 40 to report any substantial departures from the Guidelines discovered whilst carrying out work in preparation of the accountant's report. The accountant is not, however, required to determine the adequacy of a firm's interest policy (see rule 41.1(d)).

Rule 23: Amount of interest

23.1   The *interest* paid must be a fair and reasonable sum calculated over the whole period for which the money is held.

Guidance notes

(i)   You will usually account to the client for interest at the conclusion of the client's matter, but might in some cases consider it appropriate to account to the client at intervals throughout.

(ii)   The sum paid by way of interest need not necessarily reflect the highest rate of interest obtainable but it is unlikely to be appropriate to look only at the lowest rate of interest obtainable. A firm's policy on the calculation of interest will need to take into account factors such as:

(a)   the amount held;

(b)   the length of time for which cleared funds were held;

(c)   the need for instant access to the funds;

(d)   the rate of interest payable on the amount held in an instant access account at the bank or building society where the client account is kept;

(e)   the practice of the bank or building society where the client account is kept in relation to how often interest is compounded.

(iii)   A firm needs to have regard to the effect of the overall banking arrangements negotiated between it and the bank, on interest rates payable on individual balances. A fair sum of interest is unlikely to be achieved by applying interest rates which are set at an artificially low level to reflect, for example, more favourable terms in relation to the firm's office account.

(iv)   A firm might decide to apply a fixed rate of interest by reference, for example, to the base rate. In setting that rate, the firm would need to consider (and regularly review) the level of interest it actually receives on its client accounts, but also take into account its overall banking arrangements so far as they affect the rates received.

(v)   When looking at the period over which interest must be calculated, it will usually be unnecessary to check on actual clearance dates. When money is received by cheque and paid out by cheque, the normal clearance periods will usually cancel each other out, so that it will be satisfactory to look at the period between the dates when the incoming cheque is banked and the outgoing cheque is drawn.

(vi)   Different considerations apply when payments in and out are not both made by cheque. So, for example, the relevant periods would normally be:

(a)   from the date when you receive incoming money in cash until the date when the outgoing cheque is sent;

(b)   from the date when an incoming telegraphic transfer begins to earn interest until the date when the outgoing cheque is sent;

(c)   from the date when an incoming cheque or banker's draft is or would normally be cleared until the date when the outgoing telegraphic transfer is made or banker's draft is obtained.

(vii)   Rule 13.8 requires that money held in a client account must be immediately available, even at the sacrifice of interest, unless the client otherwise instructs, or the circumstances clearly indicate otherwise. The need for access can be taken into account in assessing the appropriate rate for calculating interest to be paid.

(viii)   For failure to pay a sufficient sum by way of interest, see guidance note (vi)(a) to rule 22.

Rule 24: Interest on stakeholder money

24.1   When *you* hold money as stakeholder, *you* must pay *interest* on the basis set out in rule 22 to the person to whom the stake is paid, unless the parties have contracted out of this provision (see rule 25.3).

Rule 25: Contracting out

25.1   In appropriate circumstances *you* and *your client* may by a written agreement come to a different arrangement as to the matters dealt with in rule 22 (payment of interest).

25.2   *You* must act fairly towards *your clients* when entering into an agreement to depart from the *interest* provisions, including providing sufficient information at the outset to enable them to give informed consent.

25.3   When acting as stakeholder *you* may, by a written agreement with *your* own *client* and the other party to the transaction, come to a different arrangement as to the matters dealt with in rule 22.

Guidance notes

(i)   Whether it is appropriate to contract out depends on all the circumstances, for example, the size of the sum involved or the nature, status or bargaining position of the client. It might, for instance, be appropriate to contract out by standard terms of business if the client is a substantial commercial entity and the interest involved is modest in relation to the size of the transaction. The larger the sum of interest involved, the more there would be an onus on you to show that a client who had accepted a contracting out provision was properly informed and had been treated fairly.

(ii)   Contracting out which on the face of it appears to be against the client's interests is permissible where the client has given informed consent. For example, some clients may wish to contract out for reasons related to their tax position or to comply with their religious beliefs.

(iii)   A firm which decides not to receive or pay interest, due to the religious beliefs of its principals, will need to ensure that clients are informed at the outset, so that they can choose to instruct another firm if the lack of interest is an issue for them.

(iv)   Another example of contracting out is when the client stipulates, and the firm agrees, that all interest earned should be paid to the client despite the terms of the firm's interest policy.

(v)   In principle, you are entitled to make a reasonable charge to the client for acting as stakeholder in the client's matter.

(vi)   Alternatively, it may be appropriate to include a special provision in the contract that you retain the interest on the deposit to cover your charges for acting as stakeholder. This is only acceptable if it will provide a fair and reasonable payment for the work and risk involved in holding a stake. The contract could stipulate a maximum charge, with any interest earned above that figure being paid to the recipient of the stake.

(vii)   Any right to charge the client, or to stipulate for a charge which may fall on the client, would be excluded by, for instance, a prior agreement with the client for a fixed fee for the client's matter, or for an estimated fee which cannot be varied upwards in the absence of special circumstances. It is therefore not normal practice for a stakeholder in conveyancing transactions to receive a separate payment for holding the stake.

(viii)   A stakeholder who seeks an agreement to exclude the operation of rule 24 should be particularly careful not to take unfair advantage either of the client, or of the other party if unrepresented.

PART 4: ACCOUNTING SYSTEMS AND RECORDS

Rule 26: Guidelines for accounting procedures and systems

26.1   The *SRA* may from time to time publish guidelines for accounting procedures and systems to assist *you* to comply with Parts 1 to 4 of the rules, and *you* may be required to justify any departure from the guidelines.

Guidance notes

(i)   The current guidelines appear at Appendix 3.

(ii)   The reporting accountant does not carry out a detailed check for compliance, but has a duty to report on any substantial departures from the guidelines discovered whilst carrying out work in preparation of his or her report (see rules 40 and 41.1(e)).

Rule 27: Restrictions on transfers between clients

27.1   A paper transfer of money held in a *general client account* from the ledger of one *client* to the ledger of another *client* may only be made if:

(a)   it would have been permissible to withdraw that sum from the account under rule 20.1; and

(b)   it would have been permissible to pay that sum into the account under rule 14;

(but there is no requirement in the case of a paper transfer for a written authority under rule 21.1).

27.2   No sum in respect of a *private loan* from one *client* to another can be paid out of funds held for the lender either:

(a)   by a payment from one *client account* to another;

(b)   by a paper transfer from the ledger of the lender to that of the borrower; or

(c)   to the borrower directly,

except with the prior written authority of both *clients*.

27.3   If a *private loan* is to be made by (or to) joint *clients*, the consent of each *client* must be obtained.

Rule 28: Executor, trustee or nominee companies

28.1   If *your firm* owns all the shares in a *recognised body* or a *licensed body* which is an executor, trustee or nominee company, *your firm* and the *recognised body* or *licensed body* must not operate shared *client accounts*, but may:

(a)   use one set of accounting records for money held, received or paid by the *firm* and the *recognised body* or *licensed body*; and/or

(b)   deliver a single accountant's report for both the *firm* and the *recognised body* or *licensed body*.

28.2   If such a *recognised body* or *licensed body* as nominee receives a dividend cheque made out to the *recognised body* or *licensed body*, and forwards the cheque, either endorsed or subject to equivalent instructions, to the share-owner's *bank* or *building society*, etc., the *recognised body* or *licensed body* will have received (and paid) *client money*. One way of complying with rule 29 (accounting records) is to keep a copy of the letter to the share-owner's *bank* or *building society*, etc., on the file, and, in accordance with rule 29.23, to keep another copy in a central book of such letters. (See also rule 29.17(f) (retention of records for six years)).

Rule 29: Accounting records for client accounts, etc.

Accounting records which must be kept

29.1   *You* must at all times keep accounting records properly written up to show *your* dealings with:

(a)   *client money* received, held or paid by *you*; including *client money* held outside a *client account* under rule 15.1(a) or rule 16.1(d); and

(b)   any *office money* relating to any *client* or *trust* matter.

29.2   All dealings with *client money* must be appropriately recorded:

(a)   in a client cash account or in a record of sums transferred from one client ledger account to another; and

(b)   on the client side of a separate client ledger account for each *client* (or other person, or *trust*).

No other entries may be made in these records.

29.3   If *separate designated client accounts* are used:

(a)   a combined cash account must be kept in order to show the total amount held in *separate designated client accounts*; and

(b)   a record of the amount held for each *client* (or other person, or *trust*) must be made either in a deposit column of a client ledger account, or on the client side of a client ledger account kept specifically for a *separate designated client account*, for each *client* (or other person, or *trust*).

29.4   All dealings with *office money* relating to any *client* matter, or to any *trust* matter, must be appropriately recorded in an office cash account and on the office side of the appropriate client ledger account.

29.5   A cheque or draft received on behalf of a *client* and endorsed over, not passing through a *client account*, must be recorded in the books of account as a receipt and payment on behalf of the *client*. The same applies to cash received and not deposited in a *client account* but paid out to or on behalf of a *client*.

29.6   Money which has been paid into a *client account* under rule 17.1(c) (receipt of costs), or rule 18.2(b) (mixed money), and for the time being remains in a *client account*, is to be treated as *client money*; it must be appropriately identified and recorded on the client side of the client ledger account.

29.7   Money which has been paid into an *office account* under rule 17.1(b) (receipt of costs), rule 19.1(a) (advance payments from the Legal Services Commission), or rule 19.1(b) (payment of costs from the Legal Services Commission), and for the time being remains in an *office account* without breaching the rules, is to be treated as *office money*. Money paid into an *office account* under rule 19.2(b) (regular payments) is *office money*. All these payments must be appropriately identified and recorded on the office side of the client ledger account for the individual *client* or for the Legal Services Commission.

29.8   *Client money* in a currency other than sterling must be held in a separate account for the appropriate currency, and *you* must keep separate books of account for that currency.

Current balance

29.9   The current balance on each client ledger account must always be shown, or be readily ascertainable, from the records kept in accordance with rule 29.2 and 29.3 above.

Acting for both lender and borrower

29.10   When acting for both lender and borrower on a mortgage advance, separate client ledger accounts for both *clients* need not be opened, provided that:

   (a)   the funds belonging to each *client* are clearly identifiable; and

   (b)   the lender is an institutional lender which provides mortgages on standard terms in the normal course of its activities.

Statements from banks, building societies and other financial institutions

29.11   *You* must, at least every 5 weeks:

   (a)   obtain hard copy statements (or duplicate statements permitted in lieu of the originals by rule 9.3 or 9.4 from *banks, building societies* or other financial institutions, or

   (b)   obtain and save in the *firm's* accounting records, in a format which cannot be altered, an electronic version of the *bank's, building society's* or other financial institution's on-line record,

in respect of:

   (i)   any *general client account* or *separate designated client account*;

   (ii)   any joint account held under rule 9;

   (iii) any account which is not a *client account* but in which *you* hold *client money* under rule 15.1(a) or rule 16.1(d); and

   (iv)   any *office account* maintained in relation to the *firm*;

and each statement or electronic version must begin at the end of the previous statement.

This provision does not apply in respect of passbook-operated accounts, nor in respect of the *office accounts* of an *MDP* operated solely for activities not subject to *SRA* regulation.

Reconciliations

29.12   *You* must, at least once every five weeks:

(a)   compare the balance on the client cash account(s) with the balances shown on the statements and passbooks (after allowing for all unpresented items) of all *general client accounts* and *separate designated client accounts*, and of any account which is not a *client account* but in which *you* hold *client money* under rule 15.1(a) or rule 16.1(d), and any *client money* held by *you* in cash; and

(b)   as at the same date prepare a listing of all the balances shown by the client ledger accounts of the liabilities to *clients* (and other persons, and *trusts*) and compare the total of those balances with the balance on the client cash account; and also

(c)   prepare a reconciliation statement; this statement must show the cause of the difference, if any, shown by each of the above comparisons.

29.13   Reconciliations must be carried out as they fall due, or at the latest by the due date for the next reconciliation. In the case of a *separate designated client account* operated with a passbook, there is no need to ask the *bank*, *building society* or other financial institution for confirmation of the balance held. In the case of other *separate designated client accounts*, *you* must either obtain statements at least monthly or written confirmation of the balance direct from the *bank*, *building society* or other financial institution. There is no requirement to check that *interest* has been credited since the last statement, or the last entry in the passbook.

29.14   All shortages must be shown. In making the comparisons under rule 29.12(a) and (b), *you* must not, therefore, use credits of one *client* against debits of another when checking total client liabilities.

Bills and notifications of costs

29.15   *You* must keep readily accessible a central record or file of copies of:

(a)   all bills given or sent by *you* (other than those relating entirely to activities not regulated by the *SRA*); and

(b)   all other written notifications of *costs* given or sent by *you* (other than those relating entirely to activities not regulated by the *SRA*).

Withdrawals under rule 20.1(j)

29.16   If *you* withdraw *client money* under rule 20.1(j) *you* must keep a record of the steps taken in accordance with rule 20.2(a)–(c), together with all relevant documentation (including receipts from the charity).

Retention of records

29.17   *You* must retain for at least six years from the date of the last entry:

(a)   all documents or other records required by rule 29.1 to 29.10 and 29.12 to 29.16 above;

(b)   all statements required by rule 29.11(a) above and passbooks, as printed and issued by the *bank*, *building society* or other financial institution; and/or all on-line records obtained and saved in electronic form under rule 29.11(b) above, for:

   (i)   any *general client account* or *separate designated client account*;

   (ii)   any joint account held under rule 9;

   (iii)   any account which is not a *client account* but in which *you* hold *client money* under rule 15.1(a) or rule 16.1(d); and

   (iv)   any *office account* maintained in relation to the practice, but not the *office accounts* of an *MDP* operated solely for activities not subject to *SRA* regulation;

(c)   any records kept under rule 8 (liquidators, trustees in bankruptcy, Court of Protection deputies and trustees of occupational pension schemes) including, as printed or otherwise issued, any statements, passbooks and other accounting records originating outside *your* office;

(d)   any written instructions to withhold *client money* from a *client account* (or a copy of *your* confirmation of oral instructions) in accordance with rule 15;

(e)   any central registers kept under rule 29.19 to 29.22 below; and

(f)   any copy letters kept centrally under rule 28.2 (dividend cheques endorsed over by nominee company).

29.18   *You* must retain for at least two years:

(a)   originals or copies of all authorities, other than cheques, for the withdrawal of money from a *client account*; and

(b)   all original paid cheques (or digital images of the front and back of all original paid cheques), unless there is a written arrangement with the *bank*, *building society* or other financial institution that:

   (i)   it will retain the original cheques on *your* behalf for that period; or

   (ii)   in the event of destruction of any original cheques, it will retain digital images of the front and back of those cheques on *your* behalf for that period and will, on demand by *you*, *your* reporting accountant or the *SRA*, produce copies of the digital images accompanied, when requested, by a certificate of verification signed by an authorised officer.

(c)   The requirement to keep paid cheques under rule 29.18(b) above extends to all cheques drawn on a *client account*, or on an account in which *client money* is held outside a *client account* under rule 15.1(a) or rule 16.1(d).

(d) Microfilmed copies of paid cheques are not acceptable for the purposes of rule 29.18(b) above. If a *bank*, *building society* or other financial institution is able to provide microfilmed copies only, *you* must obtain the original paid cheques from the *bank* etc. and retain them for at least two years.

Centrally kept records for certain accounts, etc.

29.19 Statements and passbooks for *client money* held outside a *client account* under rule 15.1(a) or rule 16.1(d) must be kept together centrally, or *you* must maintain a central register of these accounts.

29.20 Any records kept under rule 8 (liquidators, trustees in bankruptcy, Court of Protection deputies and trustees of occupational pension schemes) must be kept together centrally, or *you* must maintain a central register of the appointments.

29.21 The statements, passbooks, duplicate statements and copies of passbook entries relating to any joint account held under rule 9 must be kept together centrally, or *you* must maintain a central register of all joint accounts.

29.22 A central register of all withdrawals made under rule 20.1(j) must be kept, detailing the name of the *client*, other person or *trust* on whose behalf the money is held (if known), the amount, the name of the recipient charity and the date of the payment.

29.23 If a nominee company follows the option in rule 28.2 (keeping instruction letters for dividend payments), a central book must be kept of all instruction letters to the share-owner's *bank* or *building society*, etc.

Computerisation

29.24 Records required by this rule may be kept on a computerised system, apart from the following documents, which must be retained as printed or otherwise issued:

(a) original statements and passbooks retained under rule 29.17(b) above;

(b) original statements, passbooks and other accounting records retained under rule 29.17(c) above; and

(c) original cheques and copy authorities retained under rule 29.18 above.

There is no obligation to keep a hard copy of computerised records. However, if no hard copy is kept, the information recorded must be capable of being reproduced reasonably quickly in printed form for at least six years, or for at least two years in the case of digital images of paid cheques retained under rule 29.18 above.

Suspense ledger accounts

29.25   Suspense client ledger accounts may be used only when *you* can justify their use; for instance, for temporary use on receipt of an unidentified payment, if time is needed to establish the nature of the payment or the identity of the *client*.

Guidance notes

(i)   It is strongly recommended that accounting records are written up at least weekly, even in the smallest practice, and daily in the case of larger firms.

(ii)   Rule 29.1 to 29.10 (general record-keeping requirements) and rule 29.12 (reconciliations) do not apply to:

  (a) liquidators, trustees in bankruptcy, Court of Protection deputies and trustees of occupational pension schemes operating in accordance with statutory rules or regulations under rule 8.1(i);

  (b) joint accounts operated under rule 9;

  (c) a client's own account operated under rule 10; the record-keeping requirements for this type of account are set out in rule 30;

  (d) you in your capacity as a trustee when you instruct an outside administrator to run, or continue to run, on a day-to-day basis, the business or property portfolio of an estate or trust, provided the administrator keeps and retains appropriate accounting records, which are available for inspection by the SRA in accordance with rule 31. (See also guidance note (v) to rule 21.)

(iii)   A cheque made payable to a client, which is forwarded to the client by you, is not client money and falls outside the rules, although it is advisable to record the action taken. See rule 14.2(e) for the treatment of a damages cheque, made payable to the client, which you pay into a client account under the Law Society's Conditional Fee Agreement.

(iv)   Some accounting systems do not retain a record of past daily balances. This does not put you in breach of rule 29.9.

(v)   "Clearly identifiable" in rule 29.10 means that by looking at the ledger account the nature and owner of the mortgage advance are unambiguously stated. For example, if a mortgage advance of £100,000 is received from the ABC Building Society, the entry should be recorded as "£100,000, mortgage advance, ABC Building Society". It is not enough to state that the money was received from the ABC Building Society without specifying the nature of the payment, or vice versa.

(vi)   Although you do not open a separate ledger account for the lender, the mortgage advance credited to that account belongs to the lender, not to the borrower, until completion takes place. Improper removal of these mortgage funds from a client account would be a breach of rule 20.

(vii)   Section 67 of the Solicitors Act 1974 permits a solicitor or recognised body to include on a bill of costs any disbursements which have been properly incurred but not paid before delivery of the bill, subject to those disbursements being described on the bill as unpaid.

(viii)   Rule 29.17(d) – retention of client's instructions to withhold money from a client account – does not require records to be kept centrally; however this may be prudent, to avoid losing the instructions if the file is passed to the client.

(ix)   You may enter into an arrangement whereby the bank keeps digital images of paid cheques in place of the originals. The bank should take an electronic image of the front and back of each cheque in black and white and agree to hold such images, and to make printed copies available on request, for at least two years. Alternatively, you may take and keep your own digital images of paid cheques.

(x)   Certificates of verification in relation to digital images of cheques may on occasion be required by the SRA when exercising its investigative and enforcement powers. The reporting accountant will not need to ask for a certificate of verification but will be able to rely on the printed copy of the digital image as if it were the original.

(xi)   These rules require an MDP to keep accounting records only in respect of those activities for which it is regulated by the SRA. Where an MDP acts for a client in a matter which includes activities regulated by the SRA, and activities outside the SRA's regulatory reach, the accounting records should record the MDP's dealings in respect of the SRA-regulated part of the client's matter. It may also be necessary to include in those records dealings with out-of-scope money where that money has been handled in connection with, or relates to, the SRA-regulated part of the transaction. An MDP is not required to maintain records in respect of client matters which relate entirely to activities not regulated by the SRA.

Rule 30: Accounting records for clients' own accounts

30.1   When *you* operate a *client's* own account as signatory under rule 10, *you* must retain, for at least six years from the date of the last entry, the statements or passbooks as printed and issued by the *bank*, *building society* or other financial institution, and/or the duplicate statements, copies of passbook entries and cheque details permitted in lieu of the originals by rule 10.3 or 10.4; and any central register kept under rule 30.2 below.

30.2   *You* must either keep these records together centrally, or maintain a central register of the accounts operated under rule 10.

30.3   If *you* use on-line records made available by the *bank*, *building society* or other financial institution, *you* must save an electronic version in the *firm's* accounting records in a format which cannot be altered. There is no obligation to keep a hard copy but the information recorded must be capable of being reproduced reasonably quickly in printed form for at least six years.

30.4 If, when *you* cease to operate the account, the *client* requests the original statements or passbooks, *you* must take photocopies and keep them in lieu of the originals.

30.5 This rule applies only to private practice.

PART 5: MONITORING AND INVESTIGATION BY THE SRA

Rule 31: Production of documents, information and explanations

31.1 *You* must at the time and place fixed by the *SRA* produce to any person appointed by the *SRA* any records, papers, *client* and *trust* matter files, financial accounts and other documents, and any other information, necessary to enable preparation of a report on compliance with the rules.

31.2 A requirement for production under rule 31.1 above must be in writing, and left at or sent by post or document exchange to the most recent address held by the *SRA's* Information Directorate, or sent electronically to the *firm's* e-mail or fax address, or delivered by the *SRA's* appointee. A notice under this rule is deemed to be duly served:

(a) on the date on which it is delivered to or left at *your* address;

(b) on the date on which it is sent electronically to *your* e-mail or fax address; or

(c) 48 hours (excluding Saturdays, Sundays and Bank Holidays) after it has been sent by post or document exchange.

31.3 Material kept electronically must be produced in the form required by the *SRA's* appointee.

31.4 The *SRA's* appointee is entitled to seek verification from *clients* and staff, and from the *banks*, *building societies* and other financial institutions used by *you*. *You* must, if necessary, provide written permission for the information to be given.

31.5 The *SRA's* appointee is not entitled to take original documents away but must be provided with photocopies on request.

31.6 *You* must be prepared to explain and justify any departures from the Guidelines for accounting procedures and systems published by the *SRA* (see rule 26).

31.7 Any report made by the *SRA's* appointee may, if appropriate, be sent to the Crown Prosecution Service or the Serious Fraud Office and/or used in proceedings before the Solicitors Disciplinary Tribunal. In the case of an *REL* or *RFL*, the report may also be sent to the competent authority in that lawyer's home state or states. In the case of a *solicitor* who is established in another state under the *Establishment Directive*, the report may also be sent to the competent authority in the host state. The report may also be sent to any of the accountancy bodies set out in rule 34.1(a) and/or taken into account by the *SRA* in relation to a possible disqualification of a reporting accountant under rule 34.3.

31.8   Without prejudice to rule 31.1 above, *you* must produce documents relating to any account kept by *you* at a *bank* or with a *building society*:

(a)   in connection with *your* practice; or

(b)   in connection with any *trust* of which *you* are or formerly were a *trustee*,

for inspection by a person appointed by the *SRA* for the purpose of preparing a report on compliance with the rules or on whether the account has been used for or in connection with a breach of any of the Principles or other SRA Handbook requirements made or issued by the *SRA*. Rules 31.2–31.7 above apply in relation to this paragraph in the same way as to rule 31.1.

Guidance notes

(i)   The SRA's powers override any confidence or privilege between you and the client.

(ii)   The SRA's monitoring and investigation powers are exercised by Forensic Investigations.

(iii)   The SRA will normally give a brief statement of the reasons for its investigations and inspections but not if the SRA considers that there is a risk that disclosure could:

(a)   breach any duty of confidentiality;

(b)   disclose, or risk disclosure of, a confidential source of information;

(c)   significantly increase the risk that those under investigation may destroy evidence, seek to influence witnesses, default, or abscond; or

(d)   otherwise prejudice or frustrate an investigation or other regulatory action.

PART 6: ACCOUNTANTS' REPORTS

Rule 32: Delivery of accountants' reports

32.1   If *you* have, at any time during an *accounting period*, held or received *client money*, or operated a *client's* own account as signatory, *you* must deliver to the *SRA* an accountant's report for that *accounting period* within six months of the end of the *accounting period*. This duty extends to the *directors* of a *company*, or the members of an *LLP*, which is subject to this rule.

32.2   In addition the *SRA* may require the delivery of an accountant's report in circumstances other than those set out in rule 32.1 above if the *SRA* has reason to believe that it is in the public interest to do so.

Guidance notes

(i)   Examples of situations under rule 32.2 include:

   (a) when no report has been delivered but the SRA has reason to believe that a report should have been delivered;

   (b) when a report has been delivered but the SRA has reason to believe that it may be inaccurate;

   (c) when your conduct gives the SRA reason to believe that it would be appropriate to require earlier delivery of a report (for instance three months after the end of the accounting period);

   (d) when your conduct gives the SRA reason to believe that it would be appropriate to require more frequent delivery of reports (for instance every six months);

   (e) when the SRA has reason to believe that the regulatory risk justifies the imposition on a category of firm of a requirement to deliver reports earlier or at more frequent intervals;

   (f) when a condition on a solicitor's practising certificate requires earlier delivery of reports or the delivery of reports at more frequent intervals.

(ii) For accountant's reports of limited scope see rule 8 (liquidators, trustees in bankruptcy, Court of Protection deputies and trustees of occupational pension schemes), rule 9 (joint accounts) and rule 10 (operation of a client's own account). For exemption from the obligation to deliver a report, see rule 5 (persons exempt from the rules).

(iii) The requirement in rule 32 for a registered foreign lawyer to deliver an accountant's report applies only to a registered foreign lawyer practising in one of the ways set out in paragraph (iii) of the definition of "you" in rule 2.2.

(iv) The form of report is dealt with in rule 44.

(v) When client money is held or received by an unincorporated practice, the principals in the practice will have held or received client money. A salaried partner whose name appears in the list of partners on a firm's letterhead, even if the name appears under a separate heading of "salaried partners" or "associate partners", is a principal.

(vi) In the case of an incorporated practice, it is the company or LLP (i.e. the recognised body or licensed body) which will have held or received client money. The recognised body/licensed body and its directors (in the case of a company) or members (in the case of an LLP) will have the duty to deliver an accountant's report, although the directors or members will not usually have held client money.

(vii) Assistant solicitors, consultants and other employees do not normally hold client money. An assistant solicitor or consultant might be a signatory for a firm's client account, but this does not constitute holding or receiving client money. If a client or third party hands cash to an assistant solicitor, consultant or other employee, it is the sole principal or the partners (rather than the assistant solicitor, consultant or other employee) who are regarded as having received and held the money. In the case of an incorporated practice, whether a company or an LLP, it would be the recognised body or licensed body itself which would be regarded as having held or received the money.

(viii) If, exceptionally, an assistant solicitor, consultant or other employee has a client account (as a trustee), or operates a client's own account as signatory, the assistant solicitor, consultant or other employee will have to deliver an accountant's report. The assistant solicitor, consultant or other employee can be included in the report of the practice, but will need to ensure that his or her name is added, and an explanation given.

(ix) If a cheque or draft is made out to you, and in the course of practice you endorse it over to a client or employer, you have received (and paid) client money. You will have to deliver an accountant's report, even if no other client money has been held or received.

(x) Rule 32 does not apply to a solicitor or registered European lawyer, employed as an in-house lawyer by a non-solicitor employer, who operates the account of the employer or a related body of the employer.

(xi) When only a small number of transactions is undertaken or a small volume of client money is handled in an accounting period, a waiver of the obligation to deliver a report may sometimes be granted. Applications should be made to the Information Directorate.

(xii) If a firm owns all the shares in a recognised body or licensed body which is an executor, trustee or nominee company, the firm and the recognised body/licensed body may deliver a single accountant's report (see rule 28.1(b)).

Rule 33: Accounting periods

The norm

33.1 An "accounting period" means the period for which *your* accounts are ordinarily made up, except that it must:

(a) begin at the end of the previous *accounting period*; and

(b) cover twelve months.

Rules 33.2 to 33.5 below set out exceptions.

First and resumed reports

33.2 If *you* are under a duty to deliver *your* first report, the *accounting period* must begin on the date when *you* first held or received *client money* (or operated a *client's* own account as signatory), and may cover less than twelve months.

33.3   If *you* are under a duty to deliver *your* first report after a break, the *accounting period* must begin on the date when *you* for the first time after the break held or received *client money* (or operated a *client's* own account as signatory), and may cover less than twelve months.

Change of accounting period

33.4   If *you* change the period for which *your* accounts are made up (for example, on a merger, or simply for convenience), the *accounting period* immediately preceding the change may be shorter than twelve months, or longer than twelve months up to a maximum of 18 months, provided that the *accounting period* shall not be changed to a period longer than twelve months unless the *SRA* receives written notice of the change before expiry of the deadline for delivery of the accountant's report which would have been expected on the basis of *your* old *accounting period*.

Final reports

33.5   If *you* for any reason stop holding or receiving *client money* (and operating any *client's* own account as signatory), *you* must deliver a final report. The *accounting period* must end on the date upon which *you* stopped holding or receiving *client money* (and operating any *client's* own account as signatory), and may cover less than twelve months.

Guidance notes

(i)   In the case of persons joining or leaving a continuing partnership, any accountant's report for the firm as a whole will show the names and dates of the principals joining or leaving. For a person who did not previously hold or receive client money, etc., and has become a principal in the firm, the report for the firm will represent, from the date of joining, that person's first report for the purpose of rule 33.2. For a person who was a principal in the firm and, on leaving, stops holding or receiving client money, etc., the report for the firm will represent, up to the date of leaving, that person's final report for the purpose of rule 33.5 above.

(ii)   When a partnership splits up, it is usually appropriate for the books to be made up as at the date of dissolution, and for an accountant's report to be delivered within six months of that date. If, however, the old partnership continues to hold or receive client money, etc., in connection with outstanding matters, accountant's reports will continue to be required for those matters; the books should then be made up on completion of the last of those matters and a report delivered within six months of that date. The same would be true for a sole practitioner winding up matters on retirement.

(iii)   When a practice is being wound up, you may be left with money which is unattributable, or belongs to a client who cannot be traced. It may be appropriate to apply to the SRA for authority to withdraw this money from the client account – see rule 20.1(k) and guidance note (vi)(a) to rule 20.

Rule 34: Qualifications for making a report

34.1   A report must be prepared and signed by an accountant

(a)   **who is a member of:**

(i)   the Institute of Chartered Accountants in England and Wales;

(ii)   the Institute of Chartered Accountants of Scotland;

(iii)   the Association of Chartered Certified Accountants;

(iv)   the Institute of Chartered Accountants in Ireland; or

(v)   the Association of Authorised Public Accountants; **and**

(b)   **who is also:**

(i)   an individual who is a registered auditor within the terms of section 1239 of the Companies Act 2006; or

(ii)   an employee of such an individual; or

(iii)   a *partner* in or employee of a *partnership* which is a registered auditor within the terms of section 1239 of the Companies Act 2006; or

(iv)   a director or employee of a company which is a registered auditor within the terms of section 1239 of the Companies Act 2006; or

(v)   a member or employee of an *LLP* which is a registered auditor within the terms of section 1239 of the Companies Act 2006.

34.2   An accountant is not qualified to make a report if:

(a)   at any time between the beginning of the *accounting period* to which the report relates, and the completion of the report:

(i)   he or she was a *partner* or employee, or an officer or employee (in the case of a company), or a member or employee (in the case of an *LLP*) in the *firm* to which the report relates; or

(ii)   he or she was employed by the same *non-solicitor employer* as the *solicitor* or *REL* for whom the report is being made; or

(iii)   he or she was a *partner* or employee, or an officer or employee (in the case of a company), or a member or employee (in the case of an *LLP*) in an accountancy practice which had an ownership interest in, or was part of the group structure of, the *licensed body* to which the report relates; or

(b)   he or she has been disqualified under rule 34.3 below and notice of disqualification has been given under rule 34.4 (and has not subsequently been withdrawn).

34.3   The *SRA* may disqualify an accountant from making any accountant's report if:

(a) the accountant has been found guilty by his or her professional body of professional misconduct or discreditable conduct; or

(b) the *SRA* is satisfied that *you* have not complied with the rules in respect of matters which the accountant has negligently failed to specify in a report.

In coming to a decision, the *SRA* will take into account any representations made by the accountant or his or her professional body.

34.4 Written notice of disqualification must be left at or sent by recorded delivery to the address of the accountant shown on an accountant's report or in the records of the accountant's professional body. If sent through the post, receipt will be deemed 48 hours (excluding Saturdays, Sundays and Bank Holidays) after posting.

34.5 An accountant's disqualification may be notified to any *firm* likely to be affected and may be printed in the *Society's* Gazette or other publication.

Guidance note

(i) It is not a breach of the rules for you to retain an outside accountant to write up the books of account and to instruct the same accountant to prepare the accountant's report. However, the accountant will have to disclose these circumstances in the report – see the form of report in Appendix 5.

Rule 35: Reporting accountant's rights and duties – letter of engagement

35.1 *You* must ensure that the reporting accountant's rights and duties are stated in a letter of engagement incorporating the following terms:

"In accordance with rule 35 of the SRA Accounts Rules 2011, you are instructed as follows:

(a) I/this firm/this company/this limited liability partnership recognises that, if during the course of preparing an accountant's report:

(i) you discover evidence of fraud or theft in relation to money

(A) held by a solicitor (or registered European lawyer, or registered foreign lawyer, or recognised body, or licensed body, or employee of a solicitor or registered European lawyer, or manager or employee of a recognised body or licensed body) for a client or any other person (including money held on trust), or

(B) held in an account of a client, or an account of another person, which is operated by a solicitor (or registered European lawyer, registered foreign lawyer, recognised body, licensed body, employee of a solicitor or registered European lawyer, or manager or employee of a recognised body or licensed body); or

(ii) you obtain information which you have reasonable cause to believe is likely to be of material significance in determining whether a solicitor (or registered European lawyer, or registered foreign lawyer, or recognised body, or licensed body, or employee of a solicitor or registered European lawyer, or manager or employee of a recognised body or licensed body) is a fit and proper person

(A) to hold money for clients or other persons (including money held on trust), or

(B) to operate an account of a client or an account of another person,

you must immediately give a report of the matter to the Solicitors Regulation Authority if required to do so under section 34(9) of the Solicitors Act 1974;

(b) you may, and are encouraged to, make that report without prior reference to me/this firm/this company/this limited liability partnership;

(c) you are to report directly to the Solicitors Regulation Authority should your appointment be terminated following the issue of, or indication of intention to issue, a qualified accountant's report, or following the raising of concerns prior to the preparation of an accountant's report;

(d) you are to deliver to me/this firm/this company/this limited liability partnership with your report the completed checklist required by rule 43 of the SRA Accounts Rules 2011; to retain for at least three years from the date of signature a copy of the completed checklist; and to produce the copy to the Solicitors Regulation Authority on request;

(e) you are to retain these terms of engagement for at least three years after the termination of the retainer and to produce them to the Solicitors Regulation Authority on request; and

(f) following any direct report made to the Solicitors Regulation Authority under (a) or (c) above, you are to provide to the Solicitors Regulation Authority on request any further relevant information in your possession or in the possession of your firm.

To the extent necessary to enable you to comply with (a) to (f) above, I/we waive my/the firm's/the company's/the limited liability partnership's right of confidentiality. This waiver extends to any report made, document produced or information disclosed to the Solicitors Regulation Authority in good faith pursuant to these instructions, even though it may subsequently transpire that you were mistaken in your belief that there was cause for concern."

35.2 The letter of engagement and a copy must be signed by *you* and by the accountant. *You* must keep the copy of the signed letter of engagement for at least three years after the termination of the retainer and produce it to the *SRA* on request.

35.3 The specified terms may be included in a letter from the accountant to *you* setting out the terms of the engagement but the text must be adapted appropriately. The letter must be signed in duplicate by both parties, with *you* keeping the original and the accountant the copy.

Guidance note

(i)   Any direct report by the accountant to the SRA under rule 35.1(a) or (c) should be made to the Fraud and Confidential Intelligence Bureau.

Rule 36: Change of accountant

36.1   On instructing an accountancy practice to replace that previously instructed to produce accountant's reports, *you* must immediately notify the *SRA* of the change and provide the name and business address of the new accountancy practice.

Rule 37: Place of examination

37.1   Unless there are exceptional circumstances, the place of examination of *your* accounting records, files and other relevant documents must be *your* office and not the office of the accountant. This does not prevent an initial electronic transmission of data to the accountant for examination at the accountant's office with a view to reducing the time which needs to be spent at *your* office.

Rule 38: Provision of details of bank accounts, etc.

38.1   The accountant must request, and *you* must provide, details of all accounts kept or operated by *you* in connection with *your* practice at any *bank*, *building society* or other financial institution at any time during the *accounting period* to which the report relates. This includes *client accounts*, *office accounts*, accounts which are not *client accounts* but which contain *client money*, and *clients'* own accounts operated by *you* as signatory.

Rule 39: Test procedures

39.1   The accountant must examine *your* accounting records (including statements and passbooks), *client* and *trust* matter files selected by the accountant as and when appropriate, and other relevant documents, and make the following checks and tests:

  (a)   confirm that the accounting system in every office complies with:

      (i)   rule 29 – accounting records for client accounts, etc;

      (ii)   rule 30 – accounting records for clients' own accounts;

      and is so designed that:

      (A)   an appropriate client ledger account is kept for each *client* (or other person for whom *client money* is received, held or paid) or *trust*;

      (B)   the client ledger accounts show separately from other information details of all *client money* received, held or paid on account of each *client* (or other person for whom *client money* is received, held or paid) or *trust*; and

      (C)   transactions relating to *client money* and any other money dealt with through a *client account* are recorded in the accounting records in a way which distinguishes them from transactions relating to any other money received, held or paid by *you*;

(b) make test checks of postings to the client ledger accounts from records of receipts and payments of *client money*, and make test checks of the casts of these accounts and records;

(c) compare a sample of payments into and from the *client accounts* as shown in *bank* and *building society* or other financial institutions' statements or passbooks with *your* records of receipts and payments of *client money*, including paid cheques;

(d) test check the system of recording *costs* and of making transfers in respect of *costs* from the *client accounts*;

(e) make a test examination of a selection of documents requested from *you* in order to confirm:

    (i) that the financial transactions (including those giving rise to transfers from one client ledger account to another) evidenced by such documents comply with Parts 1 and 2 of the rules, rule 27 (restrictions on transfers between clients) and rule 28 (executor, trustee or nominee companies); and

    (ii) that the entries in the accounting records reflect those transactions in a manner complying with rule 29;

(f) subject to rule 39.2 below, extract (or check extractions of) balances on the client ledger accounts during the *accounting period* under review at not fewer than two dates selected by the accountant (one of which may be the last day of the *accounting period*), and at each date:

    (i) compare the total shown by the client ledger accounts of the liabilities to the *clients* (and other persons for whom *client money* is held) and *trusts* with the cash account balance; and

    (ii) reconcile that cash account balance with the balances held in the *client accounts*, and accounts which are not *client accounts* but in which *client money* is held, as confirmed direct to the accountant by the relevant *banks, building societies* and other financial institutions;

(g) confirm that reconciliation statements have been made and kept in accordance with rule 29.12 and 29.17(a);

(h) make a test examination of the client ledger accounts to see whether payments from the *client account* have been made on any individual account in excess of money held on behalf of that *client* (or other person for whom *client money* is held) or *trust*;

(i) check the office ledgers, office cash accounts and the statements provided by the *bank, building society* or other financial institution for any *office account* maintained by *you* in connection with the practice, to see whether any *client money* has been improperly paid into an *office account* or, if properly paid into an *office account* under rule 17.1(b) or rule 19.1, has been kept there in breach of the rules;

(j)   check the accounting records kept under rule 29.17(d) and 29.19 for *client money* held outside a *client account* to ascertain what transactions have been effected in respect of this money and to confirm that the *client* has given appropriate instructions under rule 15.1(a);

(k)   make a test examination of the client ledger accounts to see whether rule 29.10 (accounting records when acting for both lender and borrower) has been complied with;

(l)   for liquidators, trustees in bankruptcy, *Court of Protection deputies* and trustees of occupational pension schemes, check that records are being kept in accordance with rule 29.15, 29.17(c) and 29.20, and cross-check transactions with *client* or *trust* matter files when appropriate;

(m) check that statements and passbooks and/or duplicate statements and copies of passbook entries are being kept in accordance with rule 29.17(b)(ii) and 29.21 (record-keeping requirements for joint accounts), and cross-check transactions with *client* matter files when appropriate;

(n)   check that statements and passbooks and/or duplicate statements, copies of passbook entries and cheque details are being kept in accordance with rule 30 (record-keeping requirements for clients' own accounts), and cross-check transactions with *client* matter files when appropriate;

(o)   for money withdrawn from *client account* under rule 20.1(j), check that records are being kept in accordance with rule 29.16, 29.17(a) and 29.22, and cross-check with *client* or *trust* matter files when appropriate;

(p)   in the case of private practice only, check that for the period which will be covered by the accountant's report the *firm* was covered for the purposes of the *SRA's* indemnity insurance rules in respect of its offices in England and Wales by:

  (i)   certificates of qualifying insurance outside the assigned risks pool; or

  (ii)   a policy issued by the assigned risks pool manager; or

  (iii) certificates of indemnity cover under the professional requirements of an *REL's* home jurisdiction in accordance with paragraph 1 of Appendix 3 to those rules, together with the *SRA's* written grant of full exemption; or

  (iv)   certificates of indemnity cover under the professional requirements of an *REL's* home jurisdiction plus certificates of a difference in conditions policy with a qualifying insurer under paragraph 2 of Appendix 3 to those rules, together with the *SRA's* written grant of partial exemption; and

(q)   ask for any information and explanations required as a result of making the above checks and tests.

Extracting balances

39.2   For the purposes of rule 39.1(f) above, if *you* use a computerised or mechanised system of accounting which automatically produces an extraction of all client ledger balances, the accountant need not check all client ledger balances extracted on the list produced by the computer or machine against the individual records of client ledger accounts, provided the accountant:

(a)   confirms that a satisfactory system of control is in operation and the accounting records are in balance;

(b)   carries out a test check of the extraction against the individual records; and

(c)   states in the report that he or she has relied on this exception.

Guidance notes

(i)   The rules do not require a complete audit of your accounts nor do they require the preparation of a profit and loss account or balance sheet.

(ii)   In making the comparisons under rule 39.1(f), some accountants improperly use credits of one client against debits of another when checking total client liabilities, thus failing to disclose a shortage. A debit balance on a client account when no funds are held for that client results in a shortage which must be disclosed as a result of the comparison.

(iii)   The main purpose of confirming balances direct with banks, etc., under rule 39.1(f)(ii) is to ensure that your records accurately reflect the sums held at the bank. The accountant is not expected to conduct an active search for undisclosed accounts.

(iv)   In checking compliance with rule 20.1(j), the accountant should check on a sample basis that you have complied with rule 20.2 and are keeping appropriate records in accordance with rule 29.16, 29.17(a) and 29.22. The accountant is not expected to judge the adequacy of the steps taken to establish the identity of, and to trace, the rightful owner of the money.

Rule 40: Departures from guidelines for accounting procedures and systems

40.1   The accountant should be aware of the *SRA's* guidelines for accounting procedures and systems (see rule 26), and must note in the accountant's report any substantial departures from the guidelines discovered whilst carrying out work in preparation of the report. (See also rule 41.1(e).)

Rule 41: Matters outside the accountant's remit

41.1   The accountant is not required:

(a)   to extend his or her enquiries beyond the information contained in the documents produced, supplemented by any information and explanations given by *you*;

(b) to enquire into the stocks, shares, other securities or documents of title held by *you* on behalf of *your clients*;

(c) to consider whether *your* accounting records have been properly written up at any time other than the time at which his or her examination of the accounting records takes place;

(d) to check compliance with the provisions in rule 22 on *interest*, nor to determine the adequacy of *your interest* policy;

(e) to make a detailed check on compliance with the guidelines for accounting procedures and systems (see rules 26 and 40); or

(f) to determine the adequacy of the steps taken under paragraphs (a) and (b) of rule 20.2.

Rule 42: Privileged documents

42.1 When acting on a *client's* instructions, *you* will normally have the right on the grounds of privilege as between *solicitor* and *client* to decline to produce any document requested by the accountant for the purposes of his or her examination. In these circumstances, the accountant must qualify the report and set out the circumstances.

Guidance note

(i) In a recognised body or licensed body with one or more managers who are not legally qualified, legal professional privilege may not attach to work which is neither done nor supervised by a legally qualified individual – see Legal Services Act 2007, section 190(3) to (7), and Schedule 22, paragraph 17.

Rule 43: Completion of checklist

43.1 The accountant should exercise his or her professional judgment in adopting a suitable "audit" programme, but must also complete and sign a checklist in the form published from time to time by the *SRA*. *You* must obtain the completed checklist, retain it for at least three years from the date of signature and produce it to the *SRA* on request.

Guidance notes

(i) The current checklist appears at Appendix 4. It is issued by the SRA to firms at the appropriate time for completion by their reporting accountants.

(ii) The letter of engagement required by rule 35 imposes a duty on the accountant to hand the completed checklist to the firm, to keep a copy for three years and to produce the copy to the SRA on request.

Rule 44: Form of accountant's report

44.1 The accountant must complete and sign his or her report in the form published from time to time by the *SRA*. An explanation of any significant difference between liabilities to *clients* and *client money* held, as identified at section 4 of the report, must be given by either the accountant or *you*.

Guidance notes

(i)   The current form of accountant's report appears at Appendix 5.

(ii)   The form of report is prepared and issued by the SRA to firms at the appropriate time for completion by their reporting accountants. Separate reports can be delivered for each principal in a partnership but most firms deliver one report in the name of all the principals. For assistant solicitors, consultants and other employees, see rule 32, guidance notes (vii) and (viii).

(iii)   An incorporated practice will deliver only one report, on behalf of the company and its directors, or on behalf of the LLP and its members – see rule 32.1.

(iv)   Although it may be agreed that the accountant send the report direct to the SRA, the responsibility for delivery is that of the firm. The form of report requires the accountant to confirm that either a copy of the report has been sent to each of the persons (including bodies corporate) to whom the report relates, or a copy of the report has been sent to a named partner on behalf of all the partners in the firm. A similar confirmation is required in respect of the directors of a recognised body/licensed body which is a company, or the members of a recognised body/ licensed body which is an LLP.

(v)   A reporting accountant is not required to report on trivial breaches due to clerical errors or mistakes in book-keeping, provided that they have been rectified on discovery and the accountant is satisfied that no client suffered any loss as a result.

(vi)   In many practices, clerical and book-keeping errors will arise. In the majority of cases these may be classified by the reporting accountant as trivial breaches. However, a "trivial breach" cannot be precisely defined. The amount involved, the nature of the breach, whether the breach is deliberate or accidental, how often the same breach has occurred, and the time outstanding before correction (especially the replacement of any shortage) are all factors which should be considered by the accountant before deciding whether a breach is trivial.

(vii)   Accountants' reports should be sent to the Information Directorate.

(viii)   For direct reporting by the accountant to the SRA in cases of concern, see rule 35 and guidance note (i) to that rule.

Rule 45: Firms with two or more places of business

45.1   If a *firm* has two or more offices:

(a)   separate reports may be delivered in respect of the different offices; and

(b) separate *accounting periods* may be adopted for different offices, provided that:

(i) separate reports are delivered;

(ii) every office is covered by a report delivered within six months of the end of its *accounting period*; and

(iii) there are no gaps between the *accounting periods* covered by successive reports for any particular office or offices.

Rule 46: Waivers

46.1 The *SRA* may waive in writing in any particular case or cases any of the provisions of Part 6 of the rules, and may revoke any waiver.

Guidance note

(i) Applications for waivers should be made to the Information Directorate. In appropriate cases, firms may be granted a waiver of the obligation to deliver an accountant's report (see rule 32, and guidance note (xi) to that rule). The circumstances in which a waiver of any other provision of Part 6 would be given must be extremely rare.

PART 7: OVERSEAS PRACTICE

Rule 47: Purpose of the overseas accounts provisions

47.1 The purpose of applying different accounts provisions to overseas practice is to ensure similar protection for *client money (overseas practice)* but by way of rules which are more adaptable to conditions in other jurisdictions.

Rule 48: Application and Interpretation

48.1 Part 7 of these rules applies to your practice from an office outside England and Wales to the extent specified in each rule in this Part. If compliance with any applicable provision of Part 7 of these rules would result in your breaching local law, you may disregard that provision to the extent necessary to comply with that local law.

48.2 In Part 7 of these rules:

AJA means the Administration of Justice Act 1985;

approved regulator means any body listed as an approved regulator in paragraph 1 of Schedule 4 to the *LSA*, or designated as an approved regulator by an order under paragraph 17 of that Schedule;

authorised body means a body that has been authorised by the *SRA* to practise as a *licensed body* or a *recognised body*;

authorised non-SRA firm means a firm which is authorised to carry on *legal activities* by an *approved regulator* other than the *SRA*;

body corporate means a company, an *LLP*, or a *partnership* which is a legal person in its own right;

BSB means the Bar Standards Board;

client account (overseas practice) means an account at a bank or similar institution, subject to supervision by a public authority, which is used only for the purpose of holding *client money (overseas practice)* and/or *trust* money, and the title or designation of which indicates that the funds in the account belong to the client or clients of a *solicitor* or *REL* or are held subject to a *trust*;

client money (overseas practice) means money received or held for or on behalf of a client or *trust* (but excluding money which is held or received by a multidisciplinary practice – a *licensed body* providing a range of different services – in relation to those activities for which it is not regulated by the *SRA*);

Establishment Directive means the Establishment of Lawyers Directive 98/5/EC;

Establishment Directive profession means any profession listed in Article 1.2(a) of the *Establishment Directive*, including a solicitor, barrister or advocate of the *UK*;

firm (overseas practice) means any business through which a *solicitor* or *REL* carries on practice other than in-house practice;

lawyer-controlled body means an *authorised body* in which *lawyers of England and Wales* constitute the national group of lawyers with the largest (or equal largest) share of control of the body either as individual *managers (overseas practice)* or by their share in the control of bodies which are *managers (overseas practice)*;

lawyer of England and Wales means a *solicitor*, or an individual who is authorised to carry on *legal activities* in England and Wales by an *approved regulator* other than the *SRA*, but excludes a member of an *Establishment Directive profession* registered with the *BSB* under the *Establishment Directive*;

legal activity has the meaning given in section 12 of the *LSA* and includes any *reserved legal activity* and any other activity which consists of the provision of legal advice or assistance, or representation in connection with the application of the law or resolution of legal disputes;

licensed body means a body licensed by the *SRA* under Part 5 of the *LSA*;

licensing authority means an *approved regulator* which is designated as a licensing authority under Part 1 of Schedule 10 to the *LSA*, and whose licensing rules have been approved for the purposes of the *LSA*;

LLP means a limited liability partnership incorporated under the Limited Liability Partnerships Act 2000;

LSA means the Legal Services Act 2007;

manager (overseas practice) means:

    (i)   a member of an *LLP*;

    (ii)   a director of a company;

    (iii) a *partner* in a *partnership*; or

    (iv) in relation to any other body, a member of its governing body;

non-lawyer means:

    (i)   an individual who is not a lawyer practising as such; or

    (ii) a *body corporate* or *partnership* which is not:

        (A) an *authorised body*;

        (B) an *authorised non-SRA firm*; or

        (C) a business, carrying on the practice of lawyers from an office or offices outside England and Wales, in which a controlling majority of the *owners* and *managers* are lawyers;

owner in relation to a body, means a person with any ownership interest in the body;

partner means a person who is or is held out as a partner in a *partnership*;

partnership means an unincorporated body in which persons are or are held out as *partners*, and does not include a body incorporated as an *LLP*;

practice from an office includes practice carried on:

    (i)   from an office at which you are based; or

    (ii) from an office of a *firm (overseas practice)* in which you are the *sole practitioner*, or a *manager (overseas practice)*, or in which you have an ownership interest, even if you are not based there,

and "practising from an office" should be construed accordingly;

recognised body means a body recognised by the *SRA* under section 9 of the *AJA*;

REL means registered European lawyer, namely, an individual registered with the *SRA* under regulation 17 of the European Communities (Lawyer's Practice) Regulations 2000 (S.I. 2000 no. 1119);

REL-controlled body means an *authorised body* in which *RELs*, or *RELs* together with *lawyers of England and Wales* and/or European lawyers registered with the *BSB*, constitute the national group of lawyers with the largest (or equal largest) share of control of the body, either as individual *managers (overseas practice)* or by their share in the control of bodies which are *managers (overseas practice)*, and for this purpose *RELs* and European lawyers registered with the *BSB* belong to the national group of England and Wales;

reserved legal activity has the meaning given in section 12 of the *LSA*, and includes the exercise of a right of audience, the conduct of litigation, reserved instrument activities, probate activities, notarial activities and the administration of oaths, as defined in Schedule 2 to the *LSA*;

SA means the Solicitors Act 1974;

Society means the Law Society, in accordance with section 87 of the *SA*;

sole practitioner means a *solicitor* or *REL* practising as a sole principal, and does not include a *solicitor* or *REL* practising in-house;

solicitor means a person who has been admitted as a solicitor of the Senior Courts of England and Wales and whose name is on the roll kept by the *Society* under section 6 of the *SA*;

SRA means the Solicitors Regulation Authority, and reference to the SRA as an *approved regulator* or *licensing authority* means the SRA carrying out regulatory functions assigned to the *Society* as an *approved regulator* or *licensing authority*;

trustee includes a personal representative (i.e. an executor or an administrator), and "trust" includes the duties of a personal representative;

UK means United Kingdom.

Rule 49: Interest

49.1   You must comply with rule 49.2 below, if you hold *client money (overseas practice)* and you are:

(a)   a *solicitor sole practitioner practising from an office* outside England and Wales, or an *REL sole practitioner practising from an office* in Scotland or Northern Ireland;

(b)   a *lawyer-controlled body* or (in relation to *practice from an office* in Scotland or Northern Ireland) a *lawyer-controlled body*, or an *REL-controlled body*;

(c)   a *lawyer of England and Wales* who is a *manager (overseas practice)* of a *firm (overseas practice)* which is *practising from an office* outside the *UK*, and *lawyers of England and Wales* control the *firm (overseas practice)*, either directly as *partners*, members or *owners*, or indirectly by their ownership of *bodies corporate* which are *partners*, members or *owners*; or

(d)   a *lawyer of England and Wales* or *REL* who is a *manager (overseas practice)* of a *firm (overseas practice)* which is *practising from an office* in Scotland or Northern Ireland, and *lawyers of England and Wales* and/or *RELs* control the *firm (overseas practice)*, either directly as *partners*, members or *owners*, or indirectly by their ownership of *bodies corporate* which are *partners*, members or *owners*.

49.2   If it is fair and reasonable for interest to be earned for the client on that *client money (overseas practice)*, you must ensure that:

(a)   the *client money (overseas practice)* is dealt with so that fair and reasonable interest is earned upon it, and that the interest is paid to the client;

(b)   the client is paid a sum equivalent to the interest that would have been earned if the *client money (overseas practice)* had earned fair and reasonable interest; or

(c) any alternative written agreement with the client setting out arrangements regarding the payment of interest on that money is carried out.

49.3   In deciding whether it is fair and reasonable for interest to be earned for a client on *client money (overseas practice)*, you must have regard to all the circumstances, including:

(a) the amount of the money;

(b) the length of time for which you are likely to hold the money; and

(c) the law and prevailing custom of lawyers practising in the jurisdiction in which you are practising.

Rule 50: Accounts

Practice from an office outside the UK

50.1   You must comply with rule 50.3 and 50.4 below in relation to *practice from an office* outside the *UK* if you are:

(a) a *solicitor sole practitioner* who has held or received *client money (overseas practice)*;

(b) a *lawyer-controlled body* which has held or received *client money (overseas practice)* as a *firm (overseas practice)*;

(c) a *lawyer of England and Wales*, or a *non-lawyer*, who is a *manager (overseas practice)* of a *lawyer-controlled body* which holds or receives *client money (overseas practice)*;

(d) a *lawyer of England and Wales* who is a *manager (overseas practice)* of any other *firm (overseas practice)* which is controlled by *lawyers of England and Wales*, either directly as *partners*, members or *owners*, or indirectly by their ownership of *bodies corporate* which are *partners*, members or *owners*, if the *firm (overseas practice)* holds or receives *client money (overseas practice)*;

(e) a *solicitor* who holds or receives *client money (overseas practice)* as a named *trustee*;

(f) a *lawyer of England and Wales*, or a *non-lawyer*, who is a *manager (overseas practice)* of a *lawyer-controlled body* and who holds or receives *client money (overseas practice)* as a named *trustee*.

Practice from an office in Scotland or Northern Ireland

50.2   You must comply with rule 50.3 and 50.4 below in relation to *practice from an office* in Scotland or Northern Ireland if you are:

(a) a *solicitor* or *REL sole practitioner* who has held or received *client money (overseas practice)*;

(b) a *lawyer-controlled body*, or an *REL-controlled body*, which has held or received *client money (overseas practice)* as a *firm (overseas practice)*;

(c) a *lawyer of England and Wales*, an *REL*, a European lawyer registered with the *BSB* or a *non-lawyer*, who is a *manager (overseas practice)* of a *lawyer-controlled body*, or an *REL-controlled body*, which holds or receives *client money (overseas practice)*;

(d) a *lawyer of England and Wales* or *REL* who is a *manager (overseas practice)* of any other *firm (overseas practice)* which is controlled by *lawyers of England and Wales* and/or *RELs*, either directly as *partners*, members or *owners*, or indirectly by their ownership of *bodies corporate* which are *partners*, members or *owners*, if the *firm (overseas practice)* holds or receives *client money (overseas practice)*;

(e) a *solicitor* or *REL* who holds or receives *client money (overseas practice)* as a named *trustee*;

(f) a *lawyer of England and Wales*, a European lawyer registered with the *BSB* or a *non-lawyer*, who is a *manager (overseas practice)* of a *lawyer-controlled body*, or an *REL-controlled body*, and who holds or receives *client money (overseas practice)* as a named *trustee*.

Dealings with client money

50.3   In all dealings with *client money (overseas practice)*, you must ensure that:

(a) it is kept in a *client account (overseas practice)*, separate from money which is not *client money (overseas practice)*;

(b) on receipt, it is paid without delay into a *client account (overseas practice)* and kept there, unless the client has expressly or by implication agreed that the money shall be dealt with otherwise or you pay it straight over to a third party in the execution of a *trust* under which it is held;

(c) it is not paid or withdrawn from a *client account (overseas practice)* except:

  (i)   on the specific authority of the client;

  (ii) where the payment or withdrawal is properly required:

   (A) for a payment to or on behalf of the client;

   (B) for or towards payment of a debt due to the *firm (overseas practice)* from the client or in reimbursement of money expended by the *firm (overseas practice)* on behalf of the client; or

   (C) for or towards payment of costs due to the *firm (overseas practice)* from the client, provided that a bill of costs or other written intimation of the amount of the costs incurred has been delivered to the client and it has thereby (or otherwise in writing) been made clear to the client that the money held will be applied in payment of the costs due; or

     (iii) in proper execution of a *trust* under which it is held;

  (d) accounts are kept at all times, whether by written, electronic, mechanical or other means, to:

     (i) record all dealings with *client money (overseas practice)* in any *client account (overseas practice)*;

     (ii) show all *client money (overseas practice)* received, held or paid, distinct from any other money, and separately in respect of each client or *trust*; and

     (iii) ensure that the *firm (overseas practice)* is able at all times to account, without delay, to each and every client or *trust* for all money received, held or paid on behalf of that client or *trust*; and

  (e) all accounts, books, ledgers and records kept in relation to the *firm's (overseas practice) client account(s) (overseas practice)* are preserved for at least six years from the date of the last entry therein.

Accountants' reports

50.4   You must deliver an accountant's report in respect of any period during which you or your *firm (overseas practice)* have held or received *client money (overseas practice)* and you were subject to rule 50.3 above, within six months of the end of that period.

50.5   The accountant's report must be signed by the reporting accountant, who must be an accountant qualified in England and Wales or in the overseas jurisdiction where your office is based, or by such other person as the *SRA* may think fit. The *SRA* may for reasonable cause disqualify a person from signing accountants' reports.

50.6   The accountant's report must be based on a sufficient examination of the relevant documents to give the reporting accountant a reasonable indication whether or not you have complied with rule 50.3 above during the period covered by the report, and must include the following:

  (a) your name, practising address(es) and practising style and the name(s) of the *firm's (overseas practice) managers (overseas practice)*;

  (b) the name, address and qualification of the reporting accountant;

  (c) an indication of the nature and extent of the examination the reporting accountant has made of the relevant documents;

  (d) a statement of the total amount of money held at banks or similar institutions on behalf of clients and *trusts*, and of the total liabilities to clients and *trusts*, on any date selected by the reporting accountant (including the last day), falling within the period under review; and an explanation of any difference between the total amount of money held for clients and *trusts* and the total liabilities to clients and *trusts*;

(e) if the reporting accountant is satisfied that (so far as may be ascertained from the examination) you have complied with rule 50.3 above during the period covered by the report, except for trivial breaches, or situations where you have been bound by a local rule not to comply, a statement to that effect; and

(f) if the reporting accountant is not sufficiently satisfied to give a statement under (e) above, details of any matters in respect of which it appears to the reporting accountant that you have not complied with rule 50.3 above.

Rule 51: Production of documents, information and explanations

51.1   You must promptly comply with:

(a) a written notice from the *SRA* that you must produce for inspection by the appointee of the *SRA* all documents held by you or held under your control and all information and explanations requested:

   (i)   in connection with your practice; or

   (ii)   in connection with any *trust* of which you are, or formerly were, a *trustee*;

   for the purpose of ascertaining whether any person subject to Part 7 of these rules is complying with or has complied with any provision of this Part of these rules, or on whether the account has been used for or in connection with a breach of any of the Principles or other SRA Handbook requirements made or issued by the *SRA*; and

(b) a notice given by the *SRA* in accordance with section 44B or 44BA of the *LSA* or section 93 of the *LSA* for the provision of documents, information or explanations.

51.2   You must provide any necessary permissions for information to be given so as to enable the appointee of the *SRA* to:

(a) prepare a report on the documents produced under rule 51.1 above; and

(b) seek verification from clients, staff and the banks, building societies or other financial institutions used by you.

51.3   You must comply with all requests from the *SRA* or its appointee as to:

(a) the form in which you produce any documents you hold electronically; and

(b) photocopies of any documents to take away.

51.4   A notice under this rule is deemed to be duly served:

(a) on the date on which it is delivered to or left at your address;

(b) on the date on which it is sent electronically to your e-mail or fax address; or

(c) 48 hours (excluding Saturdays, Sundays and Bank Holidays) after it has been sent by post or document exchange to your last notified practising address.

Guidance notes

(i) If your firm has offices in and outside England and Wales, a single accountant's report may be submitted covering your practice from offices both in, and outside, England and Wales – such a report must cover compliance both with Parts 1 to 6 of these rules, and with Part 7 of these rules.

(ii) The accounting requirements and the obligation to deliver an accountant's report in this part of the rules are designed to apply to you in relation to money held or received by your firm unless it is primarily the practice of lawyers of other jurisdictions. The fact that they do not apply in certain cases is not intended to allow a lower standard of care in the handling of client money – simply to prevent the "domestic provisions" applying "by the back door" in a disproportionate or inappropriate way.

(iii) In deciding whether interest ought, in fairness, to be paid to a client, the fact that the interest is or would be negligible, or it is customary in that jurisdiction to deal with interest in a different way, may mean that interest is not payable under rule 49.2.

Rule 52: Waivers

52.1 The *SRA* may waive in writing in any particular case or cases any of the provisions of Part 7 of the rules, may place conditions on, and may revoke, any waiver.

Guidance note

(i) Applications for waivers should be made to the Professional Ethics Guidance Team. You will need to show that your circumstances are exceptional in order for a waiver to be granted.

PART 8: TRANSITIONAL PROVISIONS

Rule 53: Transitional provisions

53.1 From 31 March 2012 or the date on which an order made pursuant to section 69 of the *LSA* relating to the status of *sole practitioners* comes into force, whichever is the later, rule 2.2 of these rules shall have effect subject to the following amendments:

(a) in the definition of *non-solicitor employer*, omit the words ", *recognised sole practitioner*";

(b) omit the definition of *recognised sole practitioner*;

(c) in the definition of *you*:

    (i) in sub-paragraph (ii)(C), omit the words ", *recognised sole practitioner*" and ", or of a *sole practitioner* who should be a *recognised sole practitioner*, but has not been authorised by the *SRA*";

    (ii) in sub-paragraph (iii)(E), delete the comma and insert the word "or" between the words "*recognised body*" and "*licensed body*", and omit the words "or *recognised sole practitioner*";

(iii) for sub-paragraph (iii)(F), substitute "as an employee of a *partnership* or a *sole practitioner* which should be a *recognised body* but has not been authorised by the *SRA*";

(iv) in sub-paragraph (vi), insert the words "or a *sole practitioner*" after the word "*partnership*"; and

(v) omit sub-paragraph (vii).

53.2 With effect from the coming into force of the Order giving equivalent statutory protections to client money held by a licensed body, rule 13 shall have effect subject to the following amendments:

(a) delete rule 13.6; and

(b) in guidance note (iii) to rule 13, omit the words "of a recognised body or recognised sole practitioner" in the first sentence, and delete the second and last sentences.

53.3 These rules shall not apply to *licensed bodies* until such time as the *Society* is designated as a *licensing authority* under Part 1 of Schedule 10 to the *LSA* and all definitions shall be construed accordingly.

53.4 In these rules:

(a) references in the preamble to:

(i) the rules being made under paragraph 20 of Schedule 11 to the Legal Services Act 2007; and

(ii) licensed bodies and their managers and employees; and

(b) references to the *COFA* in rule 6 and in the Appendices;

shall have no effect until the *Society* is designated as a *licensing authority* under Part 1 of Schedule 10 to the *LSA*.

APPENDIX 1: FLOWCHART – EFFECT OF SRA ACCOUNTS RULES 2011

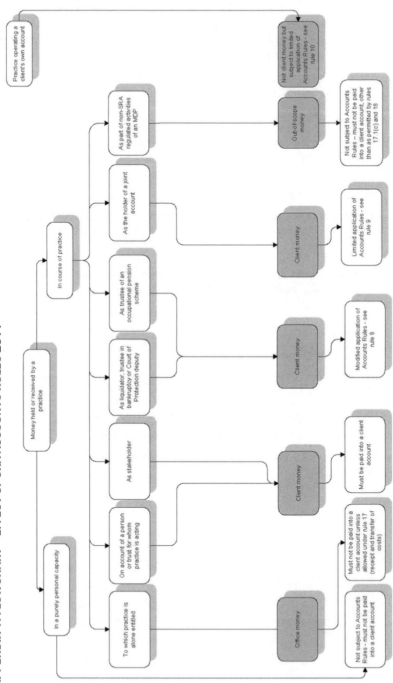

APPENDIX 2: SPECIAL SITUATIONS – WHAT APPLIES

	Is it client money?	Subject to reconciliations?	Keep books?	Retain statements?	Subject to accountant's report?	Produce records to SRA?	Interest?	Retain records generally?	Central records?	Subject to reporting accountant's comparisons?
1 R.15.1(a) a/cs in practice name (not client a/c)	Yes	Yes	Yes – r.29.1(a) and 29.2	Yes – r.29.17	Yes	Yes	Yes – r.22	Yes – r.29.17	Statements or register – r.29.19, bills – r.29.15	Yes – r.39.1(f)
2 R.15.1(b) a/cs in name of client – not operated by practice	No	No	No – record receipt and payment only	No	No	No	No – all interest earned for client – r.22, guidance note (i)(i)	No – except record of receipt and payment	Bills – r.29.15	No
3 R.15.1(b) a/cs in name of client – operated by practice	No	No	No – record receipt and payment only	Yes – r.30	Limited – r.39.1(n)	Yes – r.10	No – all interest earned for client – r.22, guidance note (i)(i)	No – except record of receipt and payment	Statements – r.30, Bills – r.29.15	No

	Is it client money?	Subject to reconciliations?	Keep books?	Retain statements?	Subject to accountant's report?	Produce records to SRA?	Interest?	Retain records generally?	Central records?	Subject to reporting accountant's comparisons?
4 Liquidators, trustees in bankruptcy and Court of Protection deputies	Yes – r.8	No – r.8	Modified – statutory records – r.8	Yes – r.8 and r.29.17(c)	Limited – r.39.1(l)	Yes – r.8	No – r.8 – comply with statutory rules (but see r.8.4 and r.22, guidance note (iv)(a))	Yes – modified r.29.17(c)	Yes – r.29.20 Bills – r.29.15	No – r.8
5 Trustees of occupational pension schemes	Yes – r.8	No – r.8	Modified – statutory records – r.8	Yes – r.8 and r.29.17(c)	Limited – r.39.1(l)	Yes – r.8	No – r.8 – comply with statutory rules (but see r.8.4 and r.22, guidance note (iv)(a))	Yes – modified r.29.17(c)	Yes – r.29.20 Bills – r.29.1	No – r.8

	Is it client money?	Subject to reconciliations?	Keep books?	Retain statements?	Subject to accountant's report?	Produce records to SRA?	Interest?	Retain records generally?	Central records?	Subject to reporting accountant's comparisons?
6 Joint accounts – r.9	Yes – r.9	No – r.9	No – r.9	Yes – r.9 and 29.17 (b)(ii)	Limited – r.39.1(m)	Yes – r.9	No. For joint a/c with client, all interest to client (r.22, guidance note (v)(a)); for joint a/c with another practice or other third party, depends on agreement	No – r.9	Statements – r.29.21 Bills – r.29.15	No – r.9
7 Acting under power of attorney	Yes	Yes	Yes	Yes	Yes	Yes	Yes	Yes	Bills – r.29.15	Yes

	Is it client money?	Subject to reconciliations?	Keep books?	Retain statements?	Subject to accountant's report?	Produce records to SRA?	Interest?	Retain records generally?	Central records?	Subject to reporting accountant's comparisons?
8 Operating client's own a/c e.g. under power of attorney – r.10	No	No	No	Yes – r.30	Limited – r.39.1(n)	Yes – r.10	No – all interest earned for client (r.22, guidance note (i)(i)	No – r.10	Statements – r.30 Bills – r.29.15	No
9 Exempt persons under r.5	No	No	No	No	No	No	No	No	No	No
10 Non-SRA regulated activities of an MDP	No – out-of-scope money – r.12	No	No – but see guidance note (xi) to r.29	No	No	Yes – r.31 – only to extent needed to check rule compliance	No	No – but see guidance note (xi) to r.29	No	No

APPENDIX 3: SRA GUIDELINES – ACCOUNTING PROCEDURES AND SYSTEMS

1. Introduction

1.1   These guidelines, published under rule 26 of the SRA Accounts Rules 2011, are intended to be a benchmark or broad statement of good practice requirements which should be present in an effective regime for the proper control of client money. They should therefore be of positive assistance to firms in establishing or reviewing appropriate procedures and systems. They do not override, or detract from the need to comply fully with, the Accounts Rules.

1.2   References to managers or firms in the guidelines are intended to include sole practitioners, recognised bodies and licensed bodies, and the managers of those bodies.

2. General

2.1   Compliance with the Accounts Rules is the equal responsibility of all managers in a firm. This responsibility also extends to the Compliance Officer for Finance and Administration, whether or not a manager (see rule 6). They should establish policies and systems to ensure that the firm complies fully with the rules, including procedures for verifying that the controls are operating effectively. Responsibility for day to day supervision may be delegated to one or more managers to enable effective control to be exercised. Delegation of total responsibility to a cashier or book-keeper is not acceptable.

2.2   The firm should hold a copy of the current version of the Accounts Rules and/or have ready access to the current on-line version. The person who maintains the books of account must have a full knowledge of the requirements of the rules and the accounting requirements of firms.

2.3   Proper books of account should be maintained on the double-entry principle. They should be legible, up to date and contain narratives with the entries which identify and/or provide adequate information about the transaction. Entries should be made in chronological order and the current balance should be shown on client ledger accounts, or be readily ascertainable, in accordance with rule 29.9.

2.4   Ledger accounts for clients, other persons or trusts should include the name of the client or other person or trust and contain a heading which provides a description of the matter or transaction.

2.5   Manual systems for recording client money are capable of complying with these guidelines. A computer system, with suitable support procedures will, however, provide an efficient means of producing the accounts and associated control information.

2.6   When introducing new systems, care must be taken to ensure:

(1)   that balances transferred from the books of account of the old system are reconciled with the opening balances held on the new system before day to day operation commences;

(2) that the new system operates correctly before the old system is abandoned. This may require a period of parallel running of the old and new systems and the satisfactory reconciliation of the two sets of records before the old system ceases.

2.7   The firm should ensure that office account entries in relation to each client or trust matter are maintained up to date as well as the client account entries. Credit balances on office account in respect of client or trust matters should be fully investigated.

2.8   The firm should establish policies and operate systems for the payment of fair and reasonable interest to clients in accordance with rules 22 and 23.

3.   Receipt of client money

3.1   The firm should have procedures for identifying client money, including cash, when received in the firm, and for promptly recording the receipt of the money either in the books of account or a register for later posting to the client cash book and ledger accounts. The procedures should cover money received through the post, electronically or direct by fee earners or other personnel. They should also cover the safekeeping of money prior to payment to bank.

3.2   The firm should have a system which ensures that client money is paid promptly into a client account.

3.3   The firm should have a system for identifying money which should not be in a client account and for transferring it without delay.

3.4   The firm should determine a policy and operate a system for dealing with money which is a mixture of office money and client money, or client money and out-of-scope money, or client money, out-of-scope money and office money, in compliance with rules 17–19.

4.   Payments from client account

4.1   The firm should have clear procedures for ensuring that all withdrawals from client accounts are properly authorised. In particular, suitable persons should be named for the following purposes:

(1) authorisation of internal payment vouchers;

(2) signing client account cheques;

(3) authorising telegraphic or electronic transfers.

No other personnel should be allowed to authorise or sign the documents.

4.2   The firm should establish clear procedures and systems for ensuring that persons permitted to authorise the withdrawal of client money from a client account have an appropriate understanding of the requirements of the rules, including rules 20 and 21 which set out when and how a withdrawal from client account may properly be made.

4.3   Persons nominated for the purpose of authorising internal payment vouchers should, for each payment, ensure there is supporting evidence showing clearly the reason for the payment, and the date of it. Similarly, persons signing cheques and authorising transfers should ensure there is a suitable voucher or other supporting evidence to support the payment.

4.4   The firm should have clear systems and procedures for authorising withdrawals from client accounts by electronic means, with appropriate safeguards and controls to ensure that all such withdrawals are properly authorised.

4.5   The firm should have a system for checking the balances on client ledger accounts to ensure no debit balances occur. Where payments are to be made other than out of cleared funds, clear policies and procedures must be in place to ensure that adequate risk assessment is applied.

N.B. If incoming payments are ultimately dishonoured, a debit balance will arise, in breach of the rules, and full replacement of the shortfall will be required under rule 7. See also rule 20, guidance notes (iii)(a) and (iv)(a).

4.6   The firm should establish systems for the transfer of costs from client account to office account in accordance with rule 17.2 and 17.3. Normally transfers should be made only on the basis of rendering a bill or written notification. The payment from the client account should be by way of a cheque or transfer in favour of the firm or sole principal – see rule 21.4.

4.7   The firm should establish policies and operate systems to control and record accurately any transfers between clients of the firm. Where these arise as a result of loans between clients, the written authority of both the lender and borrower must be obtained in accordance with rule 27.2.

4.8   The firm should establish policies and operate systems for the timely closure of files, and the prompt accounting for surplus balances in accordance with rule 14.3.

4.9   The firm should establish systems in accordance with rule 14.4 to keep clients (or other people on whose behalf money is held) regularly informed when funds are retained for a specified reason at the end of a matter or the substantial conclusion of a matter.

5.   Overall control of client accounts

5.1   The firm should maintain control of all its bank and building society accounts opened for the purpose of holding client money. In the case of a joint account, a suitable degree of control should be exercised.

5.2   Central records or central registers must be kept in respect of:

   (1)   accounts held for client money, which are not client accounts (rules 15.1(a), 16.1(d) and 29.19);

(2) practice as a liquidator, trustee in bankruptcy, Court of Protection deputy or trustee of an occupational pension scheme (rules 8 and 29.20);

(3) joint accounts (rules 9 and 29.21);

(4) dividend payments received by an executor, trustee or nominee company as nominee (rules 28.2 and 29.23); and

(5) clients' own accounts (rules 10, 15.1(b) and 30.3).

5.3 In addition, there should be a master list of all:

- general client accounts;
- separate designated client accounts;
- accounts held in respect of 5.2 above; and
- office accounts.

The master list should show the current status of each account; e.g. currently in operation or closed with date of closure.

5.4 The firm should operate a system to ensure that accurate reconciliations of the client accounts are carried out at least every five weeks. In particular it should ensure that:

(1) a full list of client ledger balances is produced. Any debit balances should be listed, fully investigated and rectified immediately. The total of any debit balances cannot be "netted off" against the total of credit balances;

(2) a full list of unpresented cheques is produced;

(3) a list of outstanding lodgements is produced;

(4) formal statements are produced reconciling the client account cash book balances, aggregate client ledger balances and the client bank accounts. All unresolved differences must be investigated and, where appropriate, corrective action taken;

(5) a manager or the Compliance Officer for Finance and Administration checks the reconciliation statement and any corrective action, and ensures that enquiries are made into any unusual or apparently unsatisfactory items or still unresolved matters.

5.5 The firm should have clear policies, systems and procedures to control access to computerised client accounts by determining the personnel who should have "write to" and "read only" access. Passwords should be held confidentially by designated personnel and changed regularly to maintain security. Access to the system should not unreasonably be restricted to a single person nor should more people than necessary be given access.

5.6 The firm should establish policies and systems for the retention of the accounting records to ensure:

- books of account, reconciliations, bills, bank statements and passbooks are kept for at least 6 years;

- paid cheques, digital images of paid cheques and other authorities for the withdrawal of money from a client account are kept for at least 2 years;

- other vouchers and internal expenditure authorisation documents relating directly to entries in the client account books are kept for at least two years.

5.7   The firm should ensure that unused client account cheques are stored securely to prevent unauthorised access. Blank cheques should not be pre-signed. Any cancelled cheques should be retained.

APPENDIX 4: REPORTING ACCOUNTANT'S CHECKLIST

[Any checks made in respect of the period [   ] to 5 October 2011 relate to compliance with the Solicitors' Accounts Rules 1998.]

The following items have been tested to satisfy the examination requirements under rules 38-40, with the results as indicated. Where the position has been found to be unsatisfactory as a result of these tests, further details have been reported in section 6 of this checklist or reported by separate appendix.

Name of practice

Results of test checks:

1. For all client money		Were any breaches discovered? (Tick the appropriate column.)		If "yes" should breaches be noted in the accountant's report?		Cross reference to audit file documentation.
(a)	**Book-keeping system for every office:**	Yes	No	Yes	No	
(i)	The accounting records satisfactorily distinguish client money from all other money dealt with by the firm.					
(ii)	A separate ledger account is maintained for each client and trust (excepting section (I) below) and the particulars of all client money received, held or paid on account of each client and trust, including funds held on separate designated deposits, or elsewhere, are recorded.					
(iii)	The client ledgers for clients and trusts show a current balance at all times, or the current balance is readily ascertainable.					
(iv)	A record of all bills of costs and written notifications has been maintained, either in the form of a central record or a file of copies of such bills.					
(b)	**Postings to ledger accounts and casts:**	Yes	No	Yes	No	
(i)	Postings to ledger accounts for clients and trusts from records of receipts and payments are correct.					
(ii)	Casts of ledger accounts for clients and trusts and receipts and payments records are correct.					
(iii)	Postings have been recorded in chronological sequence with the date being that of the initiation of the transaction.					
(c)	**Receipts and payments of client money:**	Yes	No	Yes	No	
(i)	Sample receipts and payments of client money as shown in bank and building society statements have been compared with the firm's records of receipts and payments of client money, and are correct.					

16/09/2011   Page 1 of 5   www.sra.org.uk

For alternative formats, email info.services@sra.org.uk or telephone 0870 606 2555.

86   SOLICITORS' ACCOUNTS MANUAL (12TH EDITION)

1. continued.....		Were any breaches discovered? (Tick the appropriate column.)		If "yes" should breaches be noted in the accountant;'s report?		Cross reference to audit file documentation.
(ii)	Sample paid cheques, or digital images of the front and back of sample paid cheques, have been obtained and details agreed to receipts and payment records.					
(d)	**System of recording costs and making transfers:**	Yes	No	Yes	No	
(i)	The firm's system of recording costs has been ascertained and is suitable.					
(ii)	Costs have been drawn only where required for or towards payment of the firm's costs where there has been sent to the client a bill of costs or other written notification of the amount of the costs.					
(e)	**Examination of documents for verification of transactions and entries in accounting records:**	Yes	No	Yes	No	
(i)	Make a test examination of a number of client and trust files.					
(ii)	All client and trust files requested for examination were made available.					
(iii)	The financial transactions as detailed on client and trust files and other documentation (including transfers from one ledger account to another) were valid and appropriately authorised in accordance with Parts 1 and 2 of the SRA Accounts Rules 2011 (AR).					
(iv)	The financial transactions evidenced by documents on the client and trust files were correctly recorded in the books of account in a manner complying with Part 4 AR.					
(f)	**Extraction of client ledger balances for clients and trusts:**	Yes	No	Yes	No	
(i)	The extraction of client ledger balances for clients and trusts has been checked for no fewer than two separate dates in the period subject to this report.					
(ii)	The total liabilities to clients and trusts as shown by such ledger accounts has been compared to the cash account balance(s) at each of the separate dates selected in (f)(i) above and agreed.					
(iii)	The cash account balance(s) at each of the dates selected has/have been reconciled to the balance(s) in client bank account and elsewhere as confirmed directly by the relevant banks and building societies.					
(g)	**Reconciliations:**	Yes	No	Yes	No	
(i)	During the accounting year under review, reconciliations have been carried out at least every five weeks.					
(ii)	Each reconciliation is in the form of a statement set out in a logical format which is likely to reveal any discrepancies.					
(iii)	Reconciliation statements have been retained.					
(iv)	On entries in an appropriate sample of reconciliation statements:	Yes	No	Yes	No	
	(A) All accounts containing client money have been included.					
	(B) All ledger account balances for clients and trusts as at the reconciliation date have been listed and totalled.					
	(C) No debit balances on ledger accounts for clients and trusts have been included in the total.					

1. continued…….		Were any breaches discovered? (Tick the appropriate column.)		If "yes" should breaches be noted in the accountant,'s report?		Cross reference to audit file documentation.
	(D) The cash account balance(s) for clients and trusts is/are correctly calculated by the accurate and up to date recording of transactions.					
	(E) The client bank account totals for clients and trusts are complete and correct being calculated by:					
	the closing balance *plus* an accurate and complete list of outstanding lodgements *less* an accurate and complete list of unpresented cheques.					
(v)	Each reconciliation selected under paragraph (iv) above has been achieved by the comparison and agreement *without adjusting or balancing entries* of: total of ledger balances for clients and trusts; total of cash account balances for clients and trusts; total of client bank accounts.					
(vi)	In the event of debit balances existing on ledger accounts for clients and trusts, the firm has investigated promptly and corrected the position satisfactorily.					
(vii)	In the event of the reconciliations selected under paragraph (iv) above not being in agreement, the differences have been investigated and corrected promptly.					
(h)	Payments of client money:	Yes	No	Yes	No	
	Make a test examination of the ledger accounts for clients and trusts in order to ascertain whether payments have been made on any individual account in excess of money held on behalf of that client or trust.					
(i)	Office accounts - client money:	Yes	No	Yes	No	
(i)	Check such office ledger and cash account and bank and building society statements as the firm maintains with a view to ascertaining whether any client money has not been paid into a client account.					
(ii)	Investigate office ledger credit balances and ensure that such balances do not include client money incorrectly held in office account.					
(j)	Client money not held in client account:	Yes	No	Yes	No	
(i)	Have sums not held on client account been identified?					
(ii)	Has the reason for holding such sums outside client account been established?					
(iii)	Has a written client agreement been made if appropriate?					
(iv)	Are central records or a central register kept for client money held outside client account on the client's instructions?					
(k)	Rule 27 - inter-client transfers:	Yes	No	Yes	No	
	Make test checks of inter-client transfers to ensure that rule 27 has been complied with.					
(l)	Rule 29.10 - acting for borrower and lender:	Yes	No	Yes	No	
	Make a test examination of the client ledger accounts in order to ascertain whether rule 29.10 AR has been complied with, where the firm acts for both borrower and lender in a conveyancing transaction.					
(m)	Rule 29.23 – executor, trustee or nominee companies:	Yes	No	Yes	No	
	Is a central book of dividend instruction letters kept?					

1. continued........	Were any breaches discovered? (Tick the appropriate column.)		If "yes" should breaches be noted in the accountant;'s report?		Cross reference to audit file documentation.
(n)	**Information and explanations:**	Yes	No	Yes	No	
	All information and explanations required have been received and satisfactorily cleared.					

2.	Liquidators, trustees in bankruptcy, Court of Protection deputies and trustees of occupational pension schemes (rule 8)	Were any breaches discovered? (Tick the appropriate column.)		If 'yes' should breaches be noted in the accountant's report?		Cross reference to audit file documentation
		Yes	No	Yes	No	
(a)	A record of all bills of costs and written notifications has been maintained, either in the form of a central record or a file of copies of such bills or notifications.					
(b)	Records kept under rule 8 including any statements, passbooks and other accounting records originating outside the firm's office have been retained.					
(c)	Records kept under rule 8 are kept together centrally, or a central register is kept of the appointments.					

3.	Joint accounts (rule 9)	Were any breaches discovered? (Tick the appropriate column.)		If 'yes' should breaches be noted in the accountant's report?		Cross reference to audit file documentation
		Yes	No	Yes	No	
(a)	A record of all bills of costs and written notifications has been maintained, either in the form of a central record or a file of copies of such bills or notifications.					
(b)	Statements and passbooks and/or duplicate statements or copies of passbook entries have been retained.					
(c)	Statements, passbooks, duplicate statements and copies of passbook entries are kept together centrally, or a central register of all joint accounts is kept.					

4.	Clients' own accounts (rule 10)	Were any breaches discovered? (Tick the appropriate column.)		If 'yes' should breaches be noted in the accountant's report?		Cross reference to audit file documentation
		Yes	No	Yes	No	
(a)	Statements and passbooks and/or duplicate statements, copies of passbook entries and cheque details have been retained					
(b)	Statements and passbooks and/or duplicate statements, copies of passbook entries and cheque details are kept together centrally, or a central register of clients' own accounts is kept.					

5.	SRA guidelines - accounting procedures and systems		
		Yes	No
	Discovery of substantial departures from the guidelines? *If "yes" please give details below.*		

6. Please give further details of unsatisfactory items below. (Please attach additional schedules as required.)

Signature	Date
Reporting Accountant	Print Name

APPENDIX 5: ACCOUNTANT'S REPORT FORM

AR1

Solicitors
Regulation
Authority

Accountant's Report Form

[For the period [   ] to 5 October 2011, this report relates to compliance with the Solicitors' Accounts Rules 1998.]

Under rule 32 of the SRA Accounts Rules 2011 (AR) an annual accountant's report is required from:

- ♦ a sole practitioner, if the practitioner or any of his or her employees have held or received client money, or operated a client's own account as signatory;

- ♦ a recognised body and its managers, if the recognised body or any of its managers or employees have held or received client money, or operated a client's own account as signatory;

- ♦ a licensed body and its managers, if the licensed body or any of its managers or employees have held or received client money, or operated a client's own account as signatory;

- ♦ a solicitor or registered European lawyer (REL) in in-house practice who has held or received client money, or operated a client's own account as signatory, unless exempt under rule 5;

- ♦ a solicitor, REL or registered foreign lawyer (RFL) who was a manager or employee of a partnership which should have been a recognised body but was not, if the partnership or any of those managers or employees held or received client money, or operated a client's own account as signatory.

A "recognised body" is a partnership, limited liability partnership (LLP) or company recognised by the SRA under section 9 of the Administration of Justice Act 1985. A "licensed body" is a body licensed by the SRA under Part 5 of the Legal Services Act 2007. A "manager" is a partner in a partnership, a member of an LLP or a director of a company. In the case of a partnership, "manager" includes any person held out as a partner, including a "salaried partner", "associate partner" or "local partner". As from 1 July 2009 a sole practitioner has to be recognised by the SRA as a "recognised sole practitioner". (With effect from 31 March 2012 or the date on which an order made pursuant to section 69 of the Legal Services Act relating to the status of sole practitioners comes into force, whichever is the later, a sole practitioner will have to be recognised by the SRA as a "recognised body".)

The managers and employees who, along with the recognised body/licensed body, must be named on a recognised body's/licensed body's report, are those who are managers as at the date the report is signed by the accountant (or were managers as at the last date on which the report should have been delivered under rule 32, if the report is signed after that date) and, in addition:

- ♦ in the case of a partnership, any person who was a manager at any time during the report period, and any person who, as an employee during that period, held or received client money (e.g. as a named trustee) or operated a client's own account as signatory;

- ♦ in the case of an LLP or company, any person who, as a manager or employee during the report period, held or received client money (e.g. as a named trustee) or operated a client's own account as signatory.

The accountant who prepares the report must be qualified under rule 34 of the AR and is required to report on compliance with Parts 1, 2 and 4 of the AR.

When a practice ceases to hold and/or receive client money (and/or to operate any client's own account as signatory), either on closure of the practice or for any other reason, the practice must deliver a final report within six months of ceasing to hold and/or receive client money (and/or to operate any client's own account as signatory), unless the SRA requires earlier delivery.

When a practice closes but the ceased practice continues to hold or receive client money during the process of dealing with outstanding costs and unattributable or unreturnable funds, the AR, including the obligation to deliver accountant's reports, will continue to apply. On ceasing to hold or receive client money, the ceased practice must deliver a final report within six months of ceasing to hold and/or receive client money, unless the SRA requires earlier delivery.

If you need any assistance completing this form please telephone the Contact Centre on 0870 606 2555 or email at contactcentre@sra.org.uk. Our lines are open from 09.00 to 17.00 Monday to Friday. Please note calls may be monitored/recorded for training purposes.

If you are calling from overseas please use +44 (0) 1527 504450. Note that reports in respect of practice from an office outside England and Wales are submitted under Part 7 of the AR. Specimen form **AR2** may be used for such reports.

1

1 Firm details Insert here all names used by the firm or in-house practice in respect of practice from the offices covered by this report. This must include the registered name of a recognised body/licensed body which is an LLP or company, and the name under which a partnership or sole practitioner is recognised.

Firm name(s) during the reporting period		Firm SRA no	
Report Period from		to	

Is this a cease to hold report?	Yes		No	

2 Firm's address(es) covered by this report All address(es) of the practice during the reporting period must be covered by an accountant's report, except those offices outside England and Wales not required under Part 7 of the SRA Accounts Rules 2011 to deliver a report.

Address(es)

Office Type (Head office / branch office)		Office Type (Head office / branch office)	

2

3 PLEASE COMPLETE ONE ONLY OF SECTIONS 3A, 3B, 3C AND 3D AS APPROPRIATE.

3A Sole practice. Please list the name of the sole practitioner and any consultant or employee who held or received client money, or operated a client's own account as signatory, during the report period.

Surname	Initials	SRA No.	Category – sole solicitor, sole REL, consultant, employee	Quote date if ceased to hold or receive client money

3B Recognised body/licensed body (partnership). Please list the names of all the "managers", whether individuals or bodies corporate, at the relevant date (date report is signed or due date for delivery); and any person who was a "manager" at any time during the report period; and any consultant or employee who held or received client money (e.g. as a named trustee), or operated a client's own account as signatory, during the report period; (see introductory notes).

Surname or corporate name	Initials	SRA No.	Category – manager, corporate manager, consultant, employee	Quote date if ceased to hold or receive client money

3

3C **Recognised body/licensed body (LLP or company).** Please list the names of all the "managers", whether individuals or bodies corporate, at the relevant date (date report is signed or due date for delivery); and any "manager", "corporate manager", consultant or employee who held or received client money (e.g. as a named trustee), or operated a client's own account as signatory, during the report period; (see introductory notes).

Surname or corporate name	Initials	SRA No.	Category – manager, corporate manager, consultant or employee	Date individual left the practice if applicable

3D **In-house practice.** Please list the name of every principal solicitor / REL who held or received client money at any time during the report period.

Surname	Initials	SRA No.	Category – solicitor, REL	Quote date if ceased to hold or receive client money

4

4 Comparison dates

The results of the comparisons required under rule 39.1(f) of the SRA Accounts Rules 2011, at the dates selected by me/us were:

(a)   at   *(insert date 1)*

      (i)   Liabilities to clients and trusts (and other persons for whom client money is held) as shown by ledger accounts for client and trust matters.   £

      (ii)   Cash held in client account, and client money held in any account other than a client account, after allowances for lodgments cleared after date and for outstanding cheques.   £

      (iii) Difference between (i) and (ii) (if any).   £

(b)   at   *(insert date 2)*

      (i)   Liabilities to clients and trusts (and other persons for whom client money is held) as shown by ledger accounts for client and trust matters.   £

      (ii)   Cash held in client account, and client money held in any account other than a client account, after allowances for lodgments cleared after date and for outstanding cheques.   £

      (iii) Difference between (i) and (ii) (if any).   £

Notes:

The figure to be shown in 4(a)(i) and 4(b)(i) above is the total of credit balances, without adjustment for debit balances (unless capable of proper set off, i.e. being in respect of the same client), or for receipts and payments not capable of allocation to individual ledger accounts.

An explanation must be given for any significant difference shown at 4(a)(iii) or 4(b)(iii) – see rule 44 of the SRA Accounts Rules 2011. If appropriate, it would be helpful if the explanation is given here.

5

5 Qualified report

Have you found it necessary to make this report 'Qualified'?	No	☐	If "No" proceed to section 6
	Yes	☐	If "Yes" please complete the relevant boxes

(a) Please indicate in the space provided any matters (other than trivial breaches) in respect of which it appears to you that there has been a failure to comply with the provisions of Parts 1, 2 and 4 of the SRA Accounts Rules 2011 and, in the case of private practice only, any part of the period covered by this report for which the practice does not appear to have been covered in respect of its offices in England and Wales by the insurance/indemnity documents referred to in rule 39.1(p) of the SRA Accounts Rules 2011 *(continue on an additional sheet if necessary)*:

(b) Please indicate in the space provided any matters in respect of which you have been unable to satisfy yourself and the reasons for that inability, e.g. because a client's file is not available *(continue on an additional sheet if necessary)*.

6 Accountant details The reporting accountant must be qualified in accordance with rule 34 of the SRA Accounts Rules 2011.

Name of accountant		Professional body	
		Accountant membership/ registration number	
Recognised Supervisory Body under which individual/firm is a registered auditor		Reference number of individual/firm audit registration(s)	
Firm name			
Firm address			

6

7 Declaration

In compliance with Part 6 of the SRA Accounts Rules 2011, I/we have examined to the extent required by rule 39 of those rules, the accounting records, files and other documents produced to me/us in respect of the above practice.

In so far as an opinion can be based on this limited examination, I am/we are satisfied that during the above mentioned period the practice has complied with the provisions of Parts 1, 2 and 4 of the SRA Accounts Rules 2011 except so far as concerns:

(i)   certain trivial breaches due to clerical errors or mistakes in book-keeping, all of which were rectified on discovery and none of which, I am/we are satisfied, resulted in any loss to any client or trust; and/or

(ii) any matters detailed in section 5 of this report.

In the case of private practice only, I/we certify that, in so far as can be ascertained from a limited examination of the insurance/indemnity documents produced to me/us, the practice was covered in respect of its offices in England and Wales for the period covered by this report by the insurance/indemnity documents referred to in rule 39.1(p) of the SRA Accounts Rules 2011, except as stated in section 5 of this report.

I/we have relied on the exception contained in rule 39.2 of the SRA Accounts Rules 2011.

Rule 39.2 of the SRA Accounts Rules 2011 states: "For the purposes of rule 39.1(f) above [extraction of balances] if you use a computerised or mechanised system of accounting which automatically produces an extraction of all client ledger balances, the accountant need not check all client ledger balances extracted on the list produced by the computer or machine against the individual records of client ledger accounts, provided the accountant:

(a)   confirms that a satisfactory system of control is in operation and the accounting records are in balance;

(b)   carries out a test check of the extraction against the individual records; and

(c)   states in the report that he or she has relied on this exception."

In carrying out work in preparation of this report, I/we have discovered the following substantial departures from the SRA's current Guidelines for Accounting Procedures and Systems (*continue on an additional sheet if necessary*):

Please tick the "Yes" or "No" box for the following items (i) to (v) to show whether, so far as you are aware, the relevant statement applies in respect of yourself or any principal, director (in the case of a company), member (in the case of an LLP) or employee of your accountancy practice. *Give details if appropriate.*

		Yes	No
(i)	Any of the parties mentioned above is related to any solicitor(s)/REL(s)/RFL(s) or other manager(s) to whom this report relates.	☐	☐
(ii)	Any of the parties mentioned above normally maintained, on a regular basis, the accounting records to which this report relates.	☐	☐
(iii)	Any of the parties mentioned above, or the practice, places substantial reliance for referral of clients on the practice to which this report relates.	☐	☐
(iv)	Any of the parties mentioned above, or the practice, is a client or former client of the practice to which this report relates.	☐	☐
(v)	There are other circumstances which might affect my independence in preparing this report.	☐	☐

The information is intended to help the SRA to identify circumstances which might make it difficult to give an independent report. Answering 'Yes' to any part of this section does not disqualify the accountant from making the report.

Information within the accountant's personal knowledge should always be disclosed. Detailed investigations are not necessary but reasonable enquiries should be made of those directly involved in the work.

8

I/we have completed and signed the checklist and retained a copy. The original checklist has been sent to either each of the persons listed in Section 3 or to one of them on behalf of them all.

I/we confirm that a copy of this report has been sent to (* delete as appropriate):

(a) * Each of the persons listed in Section 3; or

(b) * The following manager in the recognised body/licensed body, on behalf of all the managers in the recognised body/licensed body:

The form should then be signed and dated. The report can be signed in the name of the firm of accountants of which the accountant is a partner (in the case of a partnership) or director (in the case of a company) or member (in the case of an LLP) or employee. Particulars of the individual accountant signing the report must be given in section 6.

Please note that if this report is not completed by an accountant with the qualifications required under rule 34 of the SRA Accounts Rules 2011 it will not be accepted and will be returned to the firm for which the report has been submitted.

Date	
Signature	
Name (Block Capitals)	

Please return this form to: Caseworking and Applications Team
                            Solicitors Regulation Authority
                            Ipsley Court
                            Berrington Close
                            Redditch
                            Worcestershire
                            B98 0TD

                    OR   DX 19114 Redditch

The reporting accountant's checklist should be retained by the practice which is the subject of the report for at least three years, and not submitted to the Solicitors Regulation Authority with this report.

9

[2] SRA Principles and Code of Conduct (extracts)

[2.1] **SRA Principles 2011**

[Last updated 6 October 2011]

PREAMBLE

The SRA Principles dated 17 June 2011 commencing 6 October 2011 made by the Solicitors Regulation Authority Board under sections 31, 79 and 80 of the Solicitors Act 1974, sections 9 and 9A of the Administration of Justice Act 1985 and section 83 of the Legal Services Act 2007, with the approval of the Legal Services Board under paragraph 19 of Schedule 4 to the Legal Services Act 2007, regulating the conduct of solicitors and their employees, registered European lawyers, recognised bodies and their managers and employees, and licensed bodies and their managers and employees.

PART 1: SRA PRINCIPLES

1: SRA Principles

These are mandatory *Principles* which apply to all.

You must:

1. uphold the rule of law and the proper administration of justice;

2. act with integrity;

3. not allow your independence to be compromised;

4. act in the best interests of each *client*;

5. provide a proper standard of service to your *clients*;

6. behave in a way that maintains the trust the public places in you and in the provision of legal services;

7. comply with your legal and regulatory obligations and deal with your regulators and ombudsmen in an open, timely and co-operative manner;

8. run your business or carry out your role in the business effectively and in accordance with proper governance and sound financial and risk management principles;

9. run your business or carry out your role in the business in a way that encourages equality of opportunity and respect for diversity; and

10. protect *client* money and *assets*.

2: SRA Principles – notes

2.1   The Principles embody the key ethical requirements on firms and individuals who are involved in the provision of legal services. You should always have regard to the Principles and use them as your starting point when faced with an ethical dilemma.

2.2   Where two or more Principles come into conflict, the Principle which takes precedence is the one which best serves the public interest in the particular circumstances, especially the public interest in the proper administration of justice.

2.3   These Principles:

    (a)   apply to individuals and firms we regulate, whether traditional firms of solicitors or ABSs, in-house and overseas;

    (b)   will be breached by you if you permit another person to do anything on your behalf which if done by you would breach the Principles; and

    (c)   apply to you to the fullest extent if a sole practitioner or manager in a firm, but still apply to you if you work within a firm or in-house and have no management responsibility (for example, even if you are not a manager you may have an opportunity to influence, adopt and implement measures to comply with Principles 8 and 9).

2.4   Compliance with the Principles is also subject to any overriding legal obligations.

Principle 1: You must uphold the rule of law and the proper administration of justice.

2.5   You have obligations not only to clients but also to the court and to third parties with whom you have dealings on your clients' behalf – see, e.g., Chapter 5 (Your client and the court) and Chapter 11 (Relations with third parties) of the Code.

Principle 2: You must act with integrity.

2.6   Personal integrity is central to your role as the client's trusted adviser and should characterise all your professional dealings with clients, the court, other lawyers and the public.

Principle 3: You must not allow your independence to be compromised.

2.7   "Independence" means your own and your firm's independence, and not merely your ability to give independent advice to a client. You should avoid situations which might put your independence at risk – e.g. giving control of your practice to a third party which is beyond the regulatory reach of the SRA or other approved regulator.

Principle 4: You must act in the best interests of each client.

2.8   You should always act in good faith and do your best for each of your clients. Most importantly, you should observe:

(a) your duty of confidentiality to the client – see Chapter 4 (Confidentiality and disclosure) of the Code; and

(b) your obligations with regard to conflicts of interests – see Chapter 3 (Conflicts of interests) of the Code.

Principle 5: You must provide a proper standard of service to your clients.

2.9 You should, e.g., provide a proper standard of client care and of work. This would include exercising competence, skill and diligence, and taking into account the individual needs and circumstances of each client.

Principle 6: You must behave in a way that maintains the trust the public places in you and in the provision of legal services.

2.10 Members of the public should be able to place their trust in you. Any behaviour either within or outside your professional practice which undermines this trust damages not only you, but also the ability of the legal profession as a whole to serve society.

Principle 7: You must comply with your legal and regulatory obligations and deal with your regulators and ombudsmen in an open, timely and co-operative manner.

2.11 You should, e.g., ensure that you comply with all the reporting and notification requirements – see Chapter 10 (You and your regulator) of the Code – and respond promptly and substantively to communications.

Principle 8: You must run your business or carry out your role in the business effectively and in accordance with proper governance and sound financial and risk management principles.

2.12 Whether you are a manager or an employee, you have a part to play in helping to ensure that your business is well run for the benefit of your clients and, e.g. in meeting the outcomes in Chapter 7 (Management of your business) of the Code.

Principle 9: You must run your business or carry out your role in the business in a way that encourages equality of opportunity and respect for diversity.

2.13 Whether you are a manager or an employee, you have a role to play in achieving the outcomes in Chapter 2 (Your clients and equality and diversity) of the Code. Note that a finding of unlawful discrimination outside practice could also amount to a breach of Principles 1 and 6.

Principle 10: You must protect client money and assets.

2.14 This Principle goes to the heart of the duty to act in the best interests of your clients. You should play your part in e.g. protecting money, documents or other property belonging to your clients which has been entrusted to you or your firm.

Breach of the Principles

2.15   Our approach to enforcement is proportionate, outcomes-focused and risk-based. Therefore, how we deal with failure to comply with the Principles will depend on all the particular circumstances of each case. Our primary aim is to achieve the right outcomes for clients.

PART 2: SRA PRINCIPLES – APPLICATION PROVISIONS

The *Principles* apply to you in the following circumstances (and "you" must be construed accordingly).

3: Application of the SRA Principles in England and Wales

3.1   Subject to paragraphs 3.2 to 6.1 below and any other provisions in the *SRA Code of Conduct*, the *Principles* apply to you, in relation to your activities carried out from an office in England and Wales, if you are:

(a)   a *solicitor*, *REL* or *RFL* who is *practising* as such, whether or not the entity through which you *practise* is subject to these *Principles*;

(b)   a *solicitor*, *REL* or *RFL* who is:

   (i)   a *manager*, *employee* or *owner* of a body which should be a *recognised body*, but has not been recognised by the *SRA*;

   (ii)   a *manager*, *employee* or *owner* of a body that is a *manager* or *owner* of a body that should be a *recognised body*, but has not been recognised by the *SRA*;

   (iii)   an *employee* of a *sole practitioner* which should be a *recognised sole practitioner*, but has not been recognised by the *SRA*;

   (iv)   an *owner* of an *authorised body* or of a body which should be a *recognised body* but has not been recognised by the *SRA*, even if you undertake no work for the body's *clients*;

   (v)   a *manager* or *employee* of an *authorised non-SRA firm*, or a *manager* of a body which is a *manager* of an *authorised non-SRA firm*, when doing work of a sort authorised by the *SRA*, for that firm;

(c)   an *authorised body*, or a body which should be a *recognised body* but has not been recognised by the *SRA*;

(d)   any other person who is a *manager* or *employee* of an *authorised body*, or of a body which should be a *recognised body* but has not been recognised by the *SRA*;

(e)   any other person who is an *employee* of a *recognised sole practitioner*, or of a *sole practitioner* who should be a *recognised sole practitioner* but has not been recognised by the *SRA*;

and "you" includes "your" as appropriate.

3.2   The *Principles* apply to you if you are a *solicitor*, *REL* or *RFL*, and you are:

(a)   *practising* as a *manager* or *employee* of an *authorised non-SRA firm* when doing work of a sort authorised by the *authorised non-SRA firm's approved regulator*, or

(b)   an *owner* of an *authorised non-SRA firm* even if you undertake no work for the body's *clients*.

4: Application of the SRA Principles in relation to practice from an office outside England and Wales

4.1   The *Principles* apply to you, in relation to *practice* from an office in Scotland or Northern Ireland if you are:

(a)   a *solicitor* or an *REL practising* as such, whether or not your firm or *employer* is subject to these *Principles*;

(b)   a *lawyer-controlled body*;

(c)   an *REL-controlled body*;

(d)   any other person who is a *manager* of an *authorised body*; or

(e)   a *solicitor* who was formerly an *REL*, when *practising* as a *lawyer* of an *Establishment Directive profession*.

4.2   The *Principles* apply to you in relation to *practice* from an office outside the *UK* if you are:

(a)   a *solicitor* practising as such, whether or not your *firm* or *employer* is subject to these *Principles*;

(b)   a *lawyer-controlled body*; or

(c)   any other person who is a *manager* of an *authorised body*.

5: Application of the SRA Principles outside practice

5.1   In relation to activities which fall outside *practice*, as defined in Chapter 14 (Interpretation) of the *SRA Code of Conduct*, whether undertaken as a *lawyer* or in some other business or private capacity, *Principles* 1, 2 and 6 apply to you if you are a *solicitor*, *REL* or *RFL*.

6: General provisions

6.1   You must comply with the *Principles* at all times, but the extent to which you are expected to implement the requirements of the *Principles* will depend on your role in the *firm*, or your way of *practising*. For example, those who are managing a business will be expected to have more influence on how the *firm* or business is run than those *practising* in-house but not managing a legal department, or those *practising* as *employees* of a *firm*.

PART 3: TRANSITIONAL PROVISIONS

7: Transitional provisions

7.1   For the avoidance of doubt, where a breach of any provision of the Solicitors' Code of Conduct 2007 comes to the attention of the *SRA* after 6 October 2011, this shall be subject to action by the *SRA* notwithstanding any repeal of the relevant provision.

7.2   From 31 March 2012 or the date on which an order made pursuant to section 69 of the *LSA* relating to the status of *sole practitioners* comes into force, whichever is the later, paragraph 3.1 shall have effect subject to the following amendments:

(a)   paragraph 3.1(b) (iii) and 3.1(e) shall be omitted.

7.3   The *Principles* shall not apply to *licensed bodies* until such time as the *Society* is designated as a *licensing authority* under Part 1 of Schedule 10 to the *LSA* and all definitions shall be construed accordingly.

7.4   References in the preamble to:

(a)   the *Principles* being made under section 83 of the Legal Services Act 2007, and

(b)   *licensed bodies* and their *managers* and *employees*,

shall have no effect until such time as the *Society* is designated as a *licensing authority* under Part 1 of Schedule 10 to the *LSA*.

PART 4: INTERPRETATION

8: Interpretation

8.1   All italicised terms in these rules are to be interpreted in accordance with Chapter 14 (Interpretation) of the *SRA Code of Conduct*.

SRA Code of Conduct 2011 (extracts)

[Last updated 6 October 2011]

2ND SECTION: YOU AND YOUR BUSINESS

Chapter 7: Management of your business

This chapter is about the management and supervision of your *firm* or *in-house practice*.

Everyone has a role to play in the efficient running of a business, although of course that role will depend on the individual's position within the organisation. However, overarching responsibility for the management of the business in the broadest sense rests with the *manager(s)*. The *manager(s)* should determine what arrangements are appropriate to meet the outcomes. Factors to be taken into account will include the size and complexity of the business; the number, experience and qualifications of the *employees*; the number of offices; and the nature of the work undertaken.

Where you are using a third party to provide services that you could provide, (often described as "outsourcing"), this chapter sets out the outcomes you need to achieve.

The outcomes in this chapter show how the *Principles* apply in the context of the management of your business.

Outcomes

You must achieve these outcomes:

O(7.1)   you have a clear and effective governance structure and reporting lines;

O(7.2)   you have effective systems and controls in place to achieve and comply with all the *Principles*, rules and outcomes and other requirements of the Handbook, where applicable;

O(7.3)   you identify, monitor and manage risks to compliance with all the *Principles*, rules and outcomes and other requirements of the Handbook, if applicable to you, and take steps to address issues identified;

O(7.4)   you maintain systems and controls for monitoring the financial stability of your *firm* and risks to money and *assets* entrusted to you by *clients* and others, and you take steps to address issues identified;

O(7.5)   you comply with legislation applicable to your business, including anti-money laundering and data protection legislation;

O(7.6)   you train individuals working in the *firm* to maintain a level of competence appropriate to their work and level of responsibility;

O(7.7)   you comply with the statutory requirements for the direction and supervision of *reserved legal activities* and *immigration work*;

O(7.8)   you have a system for supervising *clients'* matters, to include the regular checking of the quality of work by suitably competent and experienced people;

O(7.9)   you do not outsource *reserved legal activities* to a *person* who is not authorised to conduct such activities;

O(7.10)   subject to Outcome 7.9, where you outsource *legal activities* or any operational functions that are critical to the delivery of any *legal activities*, you ensure such outsourcing:

  (a)   does not adversely affect your ability to comply with, or the *SRA's* ability to monitor your compliance with, your obligations in the Handbook;

  (b)   is subject to contractual arrangements that enable the *SRA* or its agent to obtain information from, inspect the records (including electronic records) of, or enter the premises of, the third party, in relation to the outsourced activities or functions;

  (c)   does not alter your obligations towards your *clients*; and

  (d)   does not cause you to breach the conditions with which you must comply in order to be authorised and to remain so.

Indicative behaviours

Acting in the following way(s) may tend to show that you have achieved these outcomes and therefore complied with the *Principles*:

IB(7.1)   safekeeping of documents and *assets* entrusted to the *firm*;

IB(7.2)   controlling budgets, expenditure and cash flow;

IB(7.3)   identifying and monitoring financial, operational and business continuity risks including *complaints*, credit risks and exposure, claims under legislation relating to matters such as data protection, IT failures and abuses, and damage to offices;

IB(7.4)   making arrangements for the continuation of your *firm* in the event of absences and emergencies, for example holiday or sick leave, with the minimum interruption to *clients'* business.

In-house practice

Outcomes 7.5 and 7.7 apply to your *in-house practice*.

Outcomes 7.1 to 7.3, and 7.6 and 7.8 to 7.10 apply to you if you have management responsibilities.

Overseas practice

The outcomes in this chapter apply to your *overseas practice*.

Notes

(i)   All of the chapters in the Code will be relevant to the management of your business, in particular those which require you to have systems and controls in place.

(ii)   This chapter should also be read with the *SRA Authorisation Rules*, the SRA Financial Services (Conduct of Business) Rules 2001 and the SRA Indemnity Insurance Rules.

3RD SECTION: YOU AND YOUR REGULATOR

Chapter 10: You and your regulator

This chapter is about co-operation with your regulators and ombudsmen, primarily the *SRA* and the *Legal Ombudsman*.

The information which we request from you will help us understand any risks to *clients*, and the public interest more generally.

The outcomes in this chapter show how the *Principles* apply in the context of you and your regulator.

Outcomes

You must achieve these outcomes:

O(10.1)   you ensure that you comply with all the reporting and notification requirements in the Handbook that apply to you;

O(10.2)   you provide the *SRA* with information to enable the *SRA* to decide upon any application you make, such as for a practising certificate, registration, recognition or a licence and whether any conditions should apply;

O(10.3)   you notify the *SRA* promptly of any material changes to relevant information about you including serious financial difficulty, action taken against you by another regulator and serious failure to comply with or achieve the *Principles*, rules, outcomes and other requirements of the Handbook;

O(10.4)   you report to the *SRA* promptly, serious misconduct by any person or *firm* authorised by the *SRA*, or any *employee*, *manager* or owner of any such *firm* (taking into account, where necessary, your duty of confidentiality to your *client*);

O(10.5)   you ensure that the *SRA* is in a position to assess whether any persons requiring prior approval are fit and proper at the point of approval and remain so;

O(10.6)   you co-operate fully with the *SRA* and the *Legal Ombudsman* at all times including in relation to any investigation about a *claim for redress* against you;

O(10.7)   you do not attempt to prevent anyone from providing information to the *SRA* or the *Legal Ombudsman*;

O(10.8)   you comply promptly with any written notice from the *SRA*;

O(10.9)   pursuant to a notice under Outcome 10.8, you:

(a)   produce for inspection by the *SRA documents* held by you, or held under your control;

(b)   provide all information and explanations requested; and

(c)   comply with all requests from the *SRA* as to the form in which you produce any *documents* you hold electronically, and for photocopies of any *documents* to take away;

in connection with your *practice* or in connection with any trust of which you are, or formerly were, a trustee;

O(10.10)   you provide any necessary permissions for information to be given, so as to enable the *SRA* to:

(a)   prepare a report on any *documents* produced; and

(b)   seek verification from *clients*, staff and the banks, building societies or other financial institutions used by you;

O(10.11) when required by the *SRA* in relation to a matter specified by the *SRA*, you:

(a)   act promptly to investigate whether any *person* may have a *claim for redress* against you;

(b)   provide the *SRA* with a report on the outcome of such an investigation, identifying *persons* who may have such a claim;

(c)   notify *persons* that they may have a right of redress against you, providing them with information as to the nature of the possible claim, about the *firm's complaints* procedure and about the *Legal Ombudsman*; and

(d)   ensure, where you have identified a *person* who may have a *claim for redress*, that the matter is dealt with under the *firm's complaints* procedure as if that *person* had made a *complaint*;

O(10.12)   you do not attempt to abrogate to any third party your regulatory responsibilities in the Handbook, including the role of Compliance Officer for Legal Practice (*COLP*) or Compliance Officer for Finance and Administration (*COFA*);

O(10.13) once you are aware that your *firm* will cease to *practise*, you effect the orderly and transparent wind-down of activities, including informing the *SRA* before the firm closes.

Indicative behaviours

Acting in the following way(s) may tend to show that you have achieved these outcomes and therefore complied with the *Principles*:

IB(10.1) actively monitoring your achievement of the outcomes in order to improve standards and identify non-achievement of the outcomes;

IB(10.2) actively monitoring your financial stability and viability in order to identify and mitigate any risks to the public;

IB(10.3) notifying the *SRA* promptly of any indicators of serious financial difficulty, such as inability to pay your professional indemnity insurance premium, or rent or salaries, or breach of bank covenants;

IB(10.4) notifying the *SRA* promptly when you become aware that your business may not be financially viable to continue trading as a going concern, for example because of difficult trading conditions, poor cash flow, increasing overheads, loss of *managers* or *employees* and/or loss of sources of revenue;

IB(10.5) notifying the *SRA* of any serious issues identified as a result of monitoring referred to in IB10.1 and IB10.2 above, and producing a plan for remedying issues that have been identified;

IB(10.6) responding appropriately to any serious issues identified concerning competence and fitness and propriety of your *employees, managers* and owners;

IB(10.7) reporting disciplinary action taken against you by another regulator;

IB(10.8) informing the *SRA* promptly when you become aware of a significant change to your *firm*, for example:

    (a) key personnel, such as a *manager, COLP* or *COFA*, joining or leaving the *firm*;

    (b) a merger with, or an acquisition by or of, another *firm*;

IB(10.9) having appropriate arrangements for the orderly transfer of *clients'* property to another *authorised body* if your *firm* closes;

IB(10.10) having a "whistle-blowing" policy.

Acting in the following way(s) may tend to show that you have not achieved these outcomes and therefore not complied with the *Principles*:

IB(10.11)   entering into an agreement which would attempt to preclude the *SRA* or the *Legal Ombudsman* from investigating any actual or potential *complaint* or allegation of professional misconduct;

IB(10.12)   unless you can properly allege malice, issuing defamation proceedings in respect of a *complaint* to the *SRA*.

In-house practice

The outcomes in this chapter apply to your *in-house practice*.

Overseas practice

The outcomes in this chapter apply to your *overseas practice*.

Notes

(i)   A notice under this chapter is deemed to be duly served:

   (a)   on the date on which it is delivered to or left at your last notified *practising* address;

   (b)   on the date on which it is sent electronically to your e-mail or fax address; or

   (c)   seven days after it has been sent by post or document exchange to your last notified *practising* address.

(ii)   The outcomes in this chapter should be considered in conjunction with the following:

   (a)   Chapter 7 (Management of your business) – requirements for risk management procedures; and

   (b)   note (xv) to Rule 8 of the *SRA Authorisation Rules*.

[3]   Annexes

Solicitors Act 1974 (ss.34, 34A, 34B and 85)

[With consolidated amendments to 1 July 2009]

34. Accountants' reports

(1)   The Society may make rules requiring solicitors to provide the Society with reports signed by an accountant (in this section referred to as an "accountant's report") at such times or in such circumstances as may be prescribed by the rules.

(2)   The rules may specify requirements to be met by, or in relation to, an accountant's report (including requirements relating to the accountant who signs the report).

(3)–(5A) [*repealed*]

(6)   If any solicitor fails to comply with the provisions of any rules made under this section, a complaint in respect of that failure may be made to the Tribunal by or on behalf of the Society.

(7)–(8) [*repealed*]

(9)   Where an accountant, during the course of preparing an accountant's report –

   (a)   discovers evidence of fraud or theft in relation to money held by a solicitor for a client or any other person (including money held on trust) or money held in an account of a client of a solicitor, or an account of another person, which is operated by the solicitor, or

   (b)   obtains information which the accountant has reasonable cause to believe is likely to be of material significance in determining whether a solicitor is a fit and proper person to hold money for clients or other persons (including money held on trust) or to operate an account of a client of the solicitor or an account of another person,

the accountant must immediately give a report of the matter to the Society.

(10)   No duty to which an accountant is subject is to be regarded as contravened merely because of any information or opinion contained in a report under subsection (9).

34A Employees of solicitors

(1)   Rules made by the Society may provide for any rules made under section 31, 32, 33A or 34 to have effect in relation to employees of solicitors with such additions, omissions or other modifications as appear to the Society to be necessary or expedient.

(2)   If any employee of a solicitor fails to comply with rules made under section 31 or 32, as they have effect in relation to the employee by virtue of subsection (1), any person may make a complaint in respect of that failure to the Tribunal.

(3)   If any employee of a solicitor fails to comply with rules made under section 34, as they have effect in relation to the employee by virtue of subsection (1), a complaint in respect of that failure may be made to the Tribunal by or on behalf of the Society.

34B   Employees of solicitors: accounts rules etc

(1)   Where rules made under section 32(1) have effect in relation to employees of solicitors by virtue of section 34A(1), section 85 applies in relation to an employee to whom the rules have effect who keeps an account with a bank or building society in pursuance of such rules as it applies in relation to a solicitor who keeps such an account in pursuance of rules under section 32.

(2)   Subsection (3) applies where rules made under section 32 –

   (a)   contain any such provision as is referred to in section 33(1), and

   (b)   have effect in relation to employees of solicitors by virtue of section 34A(1).

(3)   Except as provided by the rules, an employee to whom the rules are applied is not liable to account to any client, other person or trust for interest received by the employee on money held at a bank or building society in an account which is for money received or held for, or on account of –

   (a)   clients of the solicitor, other persons or trusts, generally, or

   (b)   that client, person or trust, separately.

(4)   Subsection (5) applies where rules made under section 33A(1) have effect in relation to employees of solicitors by virtue of section 34A(1).

(5)   The Society may disclose a report on or information about the accounts of any employee of a solicitor obtained in pursuance of such rules for use –

   (a)   in investigating the possible commission of an offence by the solicitor or any employees of the solicitor, and

   (b)   in connection with any prosecution of the solicitor or any employees of the solicitor consequent on the investigation.

(6)   Where rules made under section 34 have effect in relation to employees of solicitors by virtue of section 34A(1), section 34(9) and (10) apply in relation to such an employee as they apply in relation to a solicitor.

85.   Bank accounts

Where a solicitor keeps an account with a bank or a building society in pursuance of rules under section 32 –

(a)   the bank or society shall not incur any liability, or be under any obligation to make any inquiry, or be deemed to have any knowledge of any right of any person to any money paid or credited to the account, which it would not incur or be under or be deemed to have in the case of an account kept by a person entitled absolutely to all the money paid or credited to it; and

(b)   the bank or society shall not have any recourse or right against money standing to the credit of the account, in respect of any liability of the solicitor to the bank or society, other than a liability in connection with the account.

[3.2] Law Society's Practice Note: VAT on disbursements (extracts)

[Last updated 20 March 2011, with references to the SRA Accounts Rules 2011 in square brackets added October 2011. See **www.lawsociety.org.uk** for future updates]

Counsel's fees: concessionary treatment

A concessionary treatment for counsel's fees paid into and kept in client account was agreed between HMCE [HM Customs and Excise, the predecessor to HM Revenue and Customs], the Bar Council and the Law Society at the time VAT was first introduced (this was published in the *Gazette* on 4 April 1973).

There are two ways in which you may treat counsel's fees:

Method (i)

You may treat the fee as your own expense and thus reclaim the VAT element as input tax. When you deliver your own bill of costs to your client, the value of the supply for VAT purposes is the value of your own costs, plus the tax *exclusive* value of counsel's fees.

Example

Assume your professional charges are £1,200 plus £240 VAT (assuming a rate of 20 per cent), and the bill includes unpaid counsel's fees of £800, plus £160 VAT. The £160 VAT on counsel's fee note is treated as your input tax and can be reclaimed by you from HMRC. Your bill should show:

Legal services	£1,200.00	
Counsel's fees	£800.00	
		£2,000.00
VAT @ 20%		£400.00
TOTAL		£2,400.00

When payment of £2,400 is received, the Solicitors Accounts Rules provide that the sum may either:

* be paid into an office account at a bank or building society in England and Wales; by the end of the second working day following receipt, the amount due to counsel of £960 (£800 plus VAT of £160) must either be paid out of office account or be transferred to client account pending payment; or

* be split between client account and office account as appropriate, or be paid into client account with a transfer out of client account of office monies (£1,200 costs and £400 VAT) within 14 days of receipt.

[SRA Accounts Rules 2011, rule 17.1(b) and rule 18] – the option in rule [17.1(b)] may be used only if the payment includes no client money other than professional disbursements incurred but not yet paid.

Because counsel's fee is being treated for VAT purposes as an expense of the solicitor and the VAT element is being reclaimed by you, payment, when it is made, must be from the office account, so that the appropriate entry can be made in the VAT ledger account. At that stage the sum held in client account can be transferred to the office account.

Method (ii)

You may treat counsel's advice as supplied directly to your client and the settlement of the fees as a disbursement for VAT purposes. Counsel's VAT invoice (receipted fee note) may be amended by

- inserting on the fee note your client's name and the word "per" immediately preceding your own name and address; or

- crossing out your name and address and replacing it with the name and address of your client.

The fee note from counsel will then be recognised as a valid VAT invoice in the hands of your client (who can reclaim the VAT if registered) and no VAT record need be kept in your accounts ledgers. You should keep a photocopy of the VAT invoice.

Where you consider that the services of counsel, if supplied directly to the client, would be outside the scope of UK VAT, you must *not* certify counsel's fee note to this effect and pay counsel only the fee net of VAT. You may advise counsel that VAT is not due on their services because of the place of belonging of the client. You may provide them with appropriate commercial evidence of the client's place of belonging.

Where the client is in business in other EU Member States, this evidence could be the client's EU VAT registration number, but if no EU VAT number is provided and the client is in business in the EU, counsel should obtain commercial evidence to this effect. A statement from you that the client is in business would not be sufficient. Where the client belongs outside the EU and Isle of Man, counsel should obtain commercial evidence to confirm the place of belonging. Where no evidence of belonging is obtained, counsel should charge VAT on their services.

Example

Assuming the same level of professional charges and counsel's fees as above, your bill should show:

Legal services	£1,200.00
VAT @ 20%	£240.00
	£1,440.00
Counsel's fees (including VAT)	£960.00
TOTAL	£2,400.00

If the intention is to take advantage of the concessionary treatment and treat the supply as being made direct to your client, payment of counsel's fees must *not* be made from office account. The option in rule 19(1)(b) of paying into the office account, and then either paying counsel or transferring the amount due to the client account pending payment, cannot therefore be used.

When payment is received from your client, the cheque must either be split as to £1,440 office account and £960 client account, or alternatively the entire sum of £2,350 must be paid into the client account with a transfer out of the office monies within 14 days of receipt.

[3.3] US limited liability partnerships

[Last updated March 2009]

1. Purpose of this note

This note looks at US limited liability partnerships (LLPs) and how the Accounts Rules and the Code of Conduct affect solicitors who are partners in a US LLP.

2. The nature of US LLPs

Prior to 31 March 2009 the SRA had to distinguish for regulatory purposes between three different types of US LLP:

- an LLP which (like an English general partnership) has no separate legal personality and is simply a collection of partners carrying on business together – e.g. LLPs formed under the laws of New York State, Illinois and Georgia: "category A" LLPs;

- an LLP which has separate legal personality – e.g. LLPs formed under the laws of California, Texas, Minnesota and Washington DC: "category B" LLPs;

- an LLP which has separate legal personality but whose partners can exercise the option to negative that separate legal personality – LLPs formed under Delaware law: "category C" LLPs.

3. US LLP: practice as a recognised body in England and Wales

Before 31 March 2009, a partnership with separate legal personality committed a criminal offence under the Solicitors Act 1974 if it had an English solicitor partner and practised in England and Wales. This prevented "category B" LLPs from practising in England and Wales if they had any English solicitor partners. The same applied to a "category C" LLP with separate legal personality.

As from 31 March 2009 any US LLP with an English solicitor partner may now practise in England and Wales, provided it first obtains recognition from the SRA as a "recognised body" under section 9 of the Administration of Justice Act 1985.

Note that a US LLP is not an LLP as defined in the Solicitors' Code of Conduct 2007, the Solicitors' Accounts Rules 1998 or the Solicitors' Indemnity Insurance Rules. The rules that apply to it will be the rules applying to a partnership.

Notepaper of a US LLP practising as a recognised body in England/Wales

A US LLP which is a recognised body must have on its English notepaper a statement that it is regulated by the Solicitors Regulation Authority.

The notepaper must identify the state law under which the limited liability partnership is formed.

If there are 20 or fewer partners, the US LLP's notepaper must carry a list of the partners. If the US LLP has more than 20 partners, the notepaper must carry either a list of the partners or a statement that a list of partners is open to inspection at the office. In all cases the list must give the qualifications of all the partners:

- identifying solicitors as such;
- identifying US lawyers as US lawyers or attorneys, or naming the states in which they are qualified;
- identifying other foreign lawyers in terms of their country of qualification – and in the case of European lawyers their professional qualification in the language of their home jurisdiction;
- where practising with other English lawyers (barristers, legal executives, etc.), identifying them in terms of the profession concerned;
- where practising with non-lawyers, identifying them as non-lawyers or non-lawyer partners;
- where practising with one or more corporate partners, identifying the nature of that corporate partner if this is not clear from its name.

Compulsory professional indemnity insurance

Under the Solicitors' Indemnity Insurance Rules the US LLP must have "qualifying insurance" with a "qualifying insurer" of at least £2 million for any one claim in respect of practice carried on from the firm's office or offices in England and Wales. The only exception is that if the firm's partners include a limited company or LLP, the minimum cover required will be £3 million.

Accounts and accountant's reports

Accounts in respect of the practice of the office or offices in England and Wales must be maintained in accordance with the Solicitors' Accounts Rules 1998. Client money must be kept in a client account of the firm at a branch (or head office) in England and Wales of a bank or building society as defined in the rules. There are limited exceptions to this rule. An accountant's report on the firm's dealings with client money must be delivered to the SRA every year.

4.   US LLP: overseas branch of a recognised body

Compulsory professional indemnity insurance

If the recognised body has a branch office outside England and Wales, the Solicitors' Indemnity Insurance Rules do not apply to that office. Instead, rule 15.26 of the Code of Conduct requires solicitor partners and employees to have reasonable indemnity cover. The rule will not apply to the recognised body itself unless it is a "solicitor-controlled" recognised body.

Accounts and accountant's reports

If the recognised body has a branch office outside England and Wales, the Solicitors' Accounts Rules 1998 do not apply to that office. Accounts in respect of the recognised body's office or offices outside England and Wales will have to be maintained, and annual accountant's reports delivered, in accordance with rule 15.27 of the Code of Conduct, but only if the firm is a "solicitor-controlled" recognised body. If any solicitor partner or employee holds client money as a named trustee, accounts must be maintained and reports delivered in respect of that money, even if the firm is not a "solicitor-controlled" recognised body.

5. US LLP with no offices in England and Wales

This paragraph looks at solicitors practising as partners or employees of a US LLP with no branch offices in England and Wales. (This could be the "parent" firm which is associated with a US LLP practising as a recognised body in England and Wales.)

Compulsory professional indemnity insurance

Rule 15.26 of the Code of Conduct requires solicitor partners and employees to have reasonable indemnity cover.

Accounts and accountant's reports

Rule 15.27 of the Code of Conduct (accounts and accountant's reports for overseas offices) will not apply unless the firm is controlled by solicitors; except that if any solicitor partner or employee holds client money as a named trustee, accounts must be maintained and reports delivered in respect of that money, even if the firm is not controlled by solicitors.

[3.4] HMRC guidance: Tax on bank and building society interest

[From Business Income Manual (BIM65805), as amended on 7 June 2010. Please see guidance note (i)(d) to rule 22 of the SRA Accounts Rules 2011]

Bank and building society interest on deposits of clients' money should be dealt with as follows:

(a) Designated clients' deposit account. The client is entitled to the interest arising on the account and depending upon the status of the client the interest may be paid gross or net. The solicitor will simply pass on the interest gross or net to the client.

(b) Undesignated deposit accounts. Deduction of tax does not apply to interest on an undesignated (general) client account.

Where money is deposited into an undesignated client account the interest arises and is chargeable to the solicitor under ITTOIA/S369. At the same time the solicitor owes his or her clients an amount corresponding to the funds deposited, and will account to each client for interest thereon. Interest paid by the solicitor is chargeable on the client under ITTOIA/S369. The solicitor will be required to deduct tax only if [ITA07/S874 (1)(d)] applies, i.e. where the interest is both "yearly", and paid to a client whose usual place of abode is overseas.

The solicitor is to be assessed under ITTOIA/S369 only on the net interest retained in the year. Where the amount paid to clients exceeds the interest received the excess may be allowed as a deduction in computing the profits arising from the profession.

The tax treatment of the interest in the hands of the client is explained at SAIM2000+.